W9-ARC-438

A publication in

The NORC Series in Social Research

National Opinion Research Center

Kenneth Prewitt, Director

Improving Interview Method and Questionnaire Design

Response Effects
to Threatening Questions
in Survey Research

Norman M. Bradburn
Seymour Sudman

with the assistance of
Edward Blair
William Locander
Carrie Miles
Eleanor Singer
and Carol Stocking

Improving Interview Method and Questionnaire Design

Theodore Lownik Library
Illinois Benedictine College
Lisle, Illinois 60532

Jossey-Bass Publishers

San Francisco • Washington • London • 1980

158.3
B798i

IMPROVING INTERVIEW METHOD AND QUESTIONNAIRE DESIGN
Response Effects to Threatening Questions in Survey Research
by Norman M. Bradburn, Seymour Sudman, and Associates

Copyright © 1979 by: Jossey-Bass Inc., Publishers
433 California Street
San Francisco, California 94104
&
Jossey-Bass Limited
28 Banner Street
London EC1Y 8QE

Copyright under International, Pan American, and
Universal Copyright Conventions. All rights
reserved. No part of this book may be reproduced
in any form—except for brief quotation (not to
exceed 1,000 words) in a review or professional
work—without permission in writing from the publishers.

Library of Congress Catalogue Card Number LC 79-83569

International Standard Book Number ISBN 0-87589-402-X

Manufactured in the United States of America

JACKET DESIGN BY WILLI BAUM
FIRST EDITION
    First printing: April 1979
    Second printing: February 1980

Code 7905

The Jossey-Bass
Social and Behavioral Science Series

Preface

Improving Interview Method and Questionnaire Design presents the results of a research program on response effects in surveys conducted jointly by the National Opinion Research Center (NORC), affiliated with the University of Chicago, and the Survey Research Laboratory of the University of Illinois. This series of methodological studies follows from our review of the literature on response effects, _Response Effects in Surveys: A Review and Synthesis_ (Sudman and Bradburn, 1974), and concentrates on areas of research identified as most in need of further empirical work.

Our 1974 book developed a conceptual framework for studying response effects; we have employed this framework in the design and analysis of the methodological studies conducted since that time. In this framework, we identified three conceptually distinct causes of response effects in any given situation: variables that derive from the nature and structure of the *task*, from the characteristics of the *interviewers*, and from the characteristics of the *respondents*. The task variables were further divided into three large classes—those related (1) to the structure of the task and the method of administration, (2) to problems of self-presentation on the part of the respondent, and (3) to the saliency of the task to the respondent.

In our review we considered the effects of these task variables on three types of questions separately: nonthreatening behavioral questions, threatening behavioral questions, and attitudinal questions. For nonthreatening behavioral questions, memory factors were found to be the most important ones influencing response. Other task variables were of some importance, but interviewer and respondent demographic characteristics were of little or no importance.

For threatening behavioral questions, response effects were generally larger than for nonthreatening behavioral questions. We accounted for this difference by hypothesizing that problems of respondent self-presentation are of greater importance for threatening behavioral questions. Task variables are the most important variables influencing response, with memory variables next in importance. Respondent and interviewer variables are least important, except when either the respondents or interviewers are college students.

For attitudinal questions, task variables are also more important causes of response effects than are respondent-interviewer characteristics—except when these characteristics are highly related to the attitude being measured, as, for example, in studies of racial or sex-role attitudes. Here, saliency rather than threat seems to be the key dimension. Questions of low saliency to the respondent are subject to higher response effects.

Our recent work has been on response effects for threatening behavioral questions, and the results reported here are based on three large samples of the general population, two national and one in Chicago. For the Chicago sample, outside validation data were available for four threatening questions. For the two national studies, no outside validation was possible, but comparisons are made across alternative experimental procedures for a wide range of threatening questions. In all cases, the fieldwork was conducted by the NORC field staff. This highly select group of interviewers was able to handle the difficult experimental tasks in a thoroughly professional manner. The specific methodological details are given in the separate chapters.

Chapters One and Two deal primarily with the structure of the task and the method of administration. Chapter One compares four methods of administration: face-to-face interviews, telephone interviews, self-administered questionnaires, and randomized response. The topics range from mildly threatening, such as owning a library card, to very threatening, such as being arrested for drunken driving. Chapter Two studies the effects of question structure: the use of open and closed questions, of long and short questions, and of familiar and standard wording.

Chapters Three and Four consider interviewer effects on threatening questions. Chapter Three discusses the frequency and effect of nonprogrammed interviewer behavior, and Chapter Four studies the relatively small interviewer effects due to expectations. Chapters Five and Six explore respondent effects. Chapter Five measures the effect of acute and chronic anxiety on response, and Chapter Six evaluates using the Marlowe-Crowne scale as a measure of the social desirability effect in survey data.

Chapter Seven turns to an experiment on the effects of different introductions on response. This experiment has important implications for the current discussions on confidentiality and informed consent. Where the topics are threatening, the presence of other people can affect the answers given in an interview—the topic of Chapter Eight. Chapter Nine examines a relatively new approach—using reports of friends' behavior to obtain data, which may be more accurate than using individual reports. In Chapter Ten, we explore the problem of wording for response categories that imply some sort of quantification of responses in terms of "how much" or "how often." Chapter Eleven summarizes what we have learned from these studies and suggests avenues for future research.

Throughout the book, we attempt not only to describe and measure the response effects that are occurring but also to suggest the procedures that yield the most accurate reporting. Thus, our intended audiences are survey data collectors as well as students and researchers of response effects. While our experiments do advance our understanding of response effects, this book is clearly not intended to be the final word on this topic. As one might expect, some results are still ambiguous and need additional field research. Many of the experiments need to be repeated with different sets of threatening questions to remove epiphenomenal effects that are unique to certain topics. We hope that readers will test some of the findings given here or explore additional dimensions of response effect. Much remains to be done and the rewards are not only a better understanding of surveys but, in general, a better understanding of the social interactions between human beings.

Many of the chapters in this book are adapted from papers that have appeared in scholarly journals. The work as a whole is a truly collaborative effort, but various members of the research team have been more involved with some chapters than with others. Their respective contributions are recognized by their joint authorship of papers on which the chapters are based. We wish to thank the *Journal of the American Statistical Association,* the *Public Opinion Quarterly, The Journal of Marketing Research, The American Sociological Review,* and *Sociological Methods and Research* for their permission to reprint material from the original articles.

February 1979   Norman M. Bradburn
                                                      Chicago, Illinois
                                                      Seymour Sudman
                                                      Urbana, Illinois

Contents

xiii

The Authors

NORMAN M. BRADBURN is the Tiffany and Margaret Blake Distinguished Service Professor in the Department of Behavioral Sciences and a senior study director at the National Opinion Research Center, University of Chicago. He was awarded B.A. degrees from the University of Chicago (1952) and from Oxford University in philosophy, politics, and economics (1955). He was awarded the M.A. degree in clinical psychology (1958) and the Ph.D. degree in social psychology (1960), both from Harvard University. Since 1960, he has been on the faculty of the University of Chicago. In 1970–71 he was a Von Humboldt fellow at the University of Cologne.

Bradburn is a member of the American Sociological Association, the American Statistical Association, the American Association for Public Opinion Research, and the Council for Applied Social Research. Among the books that he has authored or coauthored are *Reports on Happiness* (with D. Caplovitz, 1965); *The Structure of Psychological Well-Being* (1969); *Side by Side* (with S. Sudman and G. Gockel, 1972); and *Response Effects in Surveys* (with S. Sudman, 1974). Bradburn continues to be engaged in research on response effects in surveys and in studies of psychological well-being.

SEYMOUR SUDMAN is professor of business administration and sociology, and research professor, Survey Research Laboratory, at the University of Illinois. He was awarded the B.S. degree in mathematics from Roosevelt University (1949) and the Ph.D. degree in business from the University of Chicago (1962). Before joining the University of Illinois in 1968, he was director of sampling and senior study director at the National Opinion Research Center, University of Chicago (1962–1968).

Sudman is a member of several professional associations, including the American Statistical Association, the American Marketing Association, and the American Sociological Association. He has written numerous books, monographs, and articles; with N. Bradburn he coauthored *Response Effects in Surveys* (1974) and published *Applied Sampling* (1976) and *Advances in Health Survey Research* (1976). He currently has two other books in press.

Improving Interview Method and Questionnaire Design

*Response Effects
to Threatening Questions
in Survey Research*

Chapter One

Effects of Question Threat and Interview Method

In the world of survey research, it is only a small exaggeration to say that methodological research on nonsampling errors is a little like the weather. Everyone talks about it, but no one does anything about it. In truth, the situation is somewhat different. There are some people, indeed a growing number, who do methodological research, but the results of their research are scattered around in a large number of journals. The amount of interesting methodological research appears to be much less than it actually is because

Note: Adapted from William Locander, Seymour Sudman, and Norman Bradburn, "An Investigation of Interview Method, Threat, and Response Distortion," *Journal of the American Statistical Association,* 1976, *71* (354), 269–275.

publication has been so widely dispersed and the research itself has rarely taken place within the context of a research program that builds on previous results.

For the past seven years, the National Opinion Research Center (NORC) affiliated with the University of Chicago and the Survey Research Laboratory (SRL) of the University of Illinois have been engaged in a series of experimental surveys to examine the effects of a variety of procedures and aspects of questionnaire construction that might affect responses in sample surveys. Based on our earlier review of the literature on response effects (Sudman and Bradburn, 1974), we felt that the most important area to investigate was that of response effects related to threatening questions, that is, questions to which respondents might respond untruthfully. Following the general practice in the field, we have published the results of these experiments in a variety of professional journals, directed to different audiences, over a number of years. It has thus been difficult for the professionally interested reader to obtain a comprehensive picture of the research and its findings. We wish to avoid adding unnecessarily to the growing body of literature on response effects, but at the same time we want to correct the impression that little serious work is being done in the area of research on nonsampling errors.

In this book we have brought together the results from three large methodological experiments conducted jointly by the staffs of NORC and SRL. By adapting the articles written for several professional journals and adding some new analyses of the data not previously published, we have tried to weave the different strands together into a coherent whole that is larger than the sum of the individual research papers. Although no single research project or even a set of projects can answer all of our methodological questions, these studies do establish a few definitive findings and lend support to particular interpretations of other results and thus contribute toward the resolution of some longstanding debates in the field.

One of the first questions that we addressed was the effects of different methods of data collection on responses. Some forms of data collection, particularly those that provided some anonymity for respondents, have long been considered most appropriate for threatening questions. Earlier studies of method of administration—such as those by Cannell and Kahn (1968), Colombotos (1969), and Enterline and Capt (1959)—suggested that this might be so, but the review by Sudman and Bradburn (1974) found no consistent or large effects. The purpose of the study described in this chapter was to examine the joint effects of question threat and method of administration on response distortion. Another major objective of this study was to analyze the randomized response model as a technique to reduce or completely eliminate response distortion on threatening or personal questions. This method has been described by Greenberg and others (1969), Horowitz, Shah, and Simmons (1967), and Warner (1965). Before proceeding to a discussion of our study, a brief description of this method is necessary to acquaint readers with it.

Random Response Model

The randomized response model was developed by Warner (1965) as a technique to reduce response distortion on threatening or personal questions. By using a probability mechanism, the respondent answers one of two questions selected randomly, but the interviewer does not know which question was answered. Generally, the respondent would answer one of the following questions "yes" or "no":

> I am a member of Group A.
> I am not a member of Group A.

By knowing the probability of answering each question, the sample size, and the total number of "yes" replies, the true proportion of the population that are members of Group A can be estimated. Warner feels that the potential advantages of the technique depend on the actual cooperation that is achieved by the model. Warner notes that the randomized response technique can be used to estimate distributions other than simple dichotomous variables. For example, estimating the proportion of a population in particular income classes can be accomplished by asking the respondent to make five separate randomized responses for each of the five classes.

Howowitz, Shah, and Simmons (1967) suggest that the technique, developed by Simmons, of using unrelated questions in the randomized response model is a valuable modification. They argue that this helps to overcome the respondent's suspicions and thus increases cooperation. With this modification, one question should be threatening, and the other should be innocuous and unrelated. The questions should read as follows:

I am a member of Group A.
I am a member of Group B.

With this method, the unrelated question data are treated as a separate sample for estimating purposes. As long as the probabilities are not equal, the sample estimate can be obtained as follows.

Given:

π_A = true proportion with attribute A
P_1 = probability that the statement "I am a member of Group A" is exposed to the respondent
$1 - P_1$ = probability that the statement "I am a member of Group B" is exposed to the respondent
π_B = true proportion with attribute B
λ_1 = proportion of "yes" answers,

the sample estimate can be determined by:

$$\pi_A = \left[\lambda_1 - \pi_B \left(1 - P_1\right)\right]/P_1 \tag{1}$$

Design of the Study

The study compared four interview techniques—face-to-face, telephone, self-administered, and the random response model. Figure 1 shows the design, including the four levels of threatening questions. It was planned that there would be fifty respondents per cell and thus a total sample size of eight hundred.

The threat dimension included questions about the ownership of a Chicago public library card, voter registration and voting behavior, involvement in bankruptcy, and being charged with drunken driving. These four topics were chosen because we believe that the level of threat increases as one proceeds from a question about having a library card to one about being charged with drun-

		Low Threat ◄————————► High Threat			
		Library Card and Voting Behavior	*Bankruptcy*	*Drunken Driving*	*N*
Highly Personal	Face-to-Face	100	50	50	200
	Telephone	100	50	50	200
	Self-Administered	100	50	50	200
Anonymous	Random Response	100	50	50	200
					800

Figure 1. Study Design: Question Threat by Method of Administration.

ken driving. In addition, it was possible to obtain validation information from public records for these questions. Thus, it is possible to see what differences there are not only by method of administration and threat but also by the actual response error. The questions are reproduced in Appendix A.

The respondents in the face-to-face bankruptcy cell had all declared bankruptcy in the recent past. The respondents in the drunken driving cells had all been charged with drunken driving not less than six months and not more than twelve months from the starting date of the study. The respondents in the library card and voting behavior cells were drawn from a household probability sample and validated from Chicago public library and city voting records. This sample was selected using random digit dialing of households with telephones. A listing of all members of the household was conducted during a screening interview, and one adult was subsequently selected at random for interviewing. The telephone sample was used to eliminate the possibility of differences in methods of administration arising from sample differences rather than response distortion. About 90 percent of Chicago households, however, do have telephones. We ignored possible errors in lists of library card holders and voters, such as misfiling or misspelling of names, since there is no reason to believe that such errors would be related to the method of administration of questions.

We recognized that our judgment of threat might not be the same as the respondent's. Admission of bankruptcy, for example, might seem highly threatening, because it could be viewed as a personal failure, but some people might see it as a shrewd business tactic to alleviate debt. After the main part of the interview was completed, respondents were asked how threatening they found the questions. The responses to these questions were combined to form an acute anxiety scale. A measure of chronic anxiety was also obtained, so that response effects could be related to chronic, acute, and total anxiety. Chronic anxiety was measured by the Bendig Short Form of the Taylor Manifest Anxiety Scale (Bendig, 1956).

The random response model was operationalized using a three-by-five-inch plastic box containing fifty beads, 70 percent red and 30 percent blue. The box was designed so that either a red or blue bead would randomly appear in a small window in the front of the mechanism. Respondents were given the box and told to make sure that they could get beads of both colors to appear in the window by shaking the box. Questions in pairs, one keyed to the red bead and one to the blue, were put on flip cards and presented by the interviewer at particular parts of the interview. Respondents were told that certain questions in survey research are difficult to ask directly. They were then directed to answer "yes" or "no" to the real or unrelated question that was chosen by the mechanism, after being assured that the interviewer did not know which question they were answering but was merely recording the "yes" or "no" response.

Interviewer assignments were randomized over the different models of administration, but interviewers were matched with respondents on race. Interviewers were not told that some of the respondents had been selected from special lists but were simply given the assignments as in a normal area probability sample. All respondents within a given treatment answered all questions.

Interview Completion Rates

The rate of completed interviews varied by method and group. Table 1 shows the percentage completed by method and sample. The overall completion rate was 72.2 percent of 941 interviews. This is about average for a sample in a large city. Use of the telephone achieved the highest interview completion rate, better than the other three methods across all sample types, except in the bankruptcy sample when compared with personal interviewing.

Table 1. Percentage of Completed Interviews and Standard Errors

Methods	Sample			
	General Sample	Bankrupts	Drunken Drivers	Total
Personal Interview	76.0	70.3	57.1	69.8
	N = 125	N = 54	N = 63	N = 242
	3.82	6.22	6.31	2.95
Telephone	89.9	68.9	77.8	81.0
	N = 109	N = 60	N = 63	N = 232
	2.89	5.98	5.24	2.58
Self-Administered	75.4	59.3	47.5	64.1
	N = 114	N = 59	N = 61	N = 234
	4.03	6.40	6.39	3.14
Random Response	77.6	67.2	58.1	70.0
	N = 116	N = 55	N = 62	N = 233
	3.87	6.33	6.27	3.0
Total	79.7	66.2	60.2	
	N = 464	N = 228	N = 249	
	1.87	3.13	3.10	

The telephone was relatively more successful in getting completed interviews with drunken drivers. The self-administered technique, where the interviewer left a questionnaire and picked it up later, was about as successful as personal interviewing and the random response model in the general sample. However, self-administration was not nearly as good for the bankruptcy and drunken driving samples, where a large fraction of the respondents had not finished high school. The random response method achieved completion rates similar to those for personal interviewing.

It was much more difficult to locate the bankrupts and drunken drivers, and this factor was the major source of incomplete interviews in these groups. About 90 percent of the noninterviews with bankrupts and 80 percent of the noninterviews with drunken drivers were due to the interviewers' inability to locate the respondent. It is typically more difficult to locate respondents from a list sample with some outdated addresses than from an area probability sample. It was also noted, however, that the drunken driving and bankrupt samples had somewhat lower average incomes and years in school. Thus, some of the results reported here might be due in part to differences in sample characteristics.

Results

The main findings of this study are shown in Table 2. The data are presented as proportions of distortion for each of the twenty cells representing different conditions. The results represent the proportion of respondents in each condition who gave incorrect answers. The proportion of distortion in each cell is defined as the difference divided by the total sample size (Formula 1):

$$\text{Distortion} = \mid \text{Response} - \text{Validated} \mid /\text{Total } N$$

It should be noted that the sample sizes in Table 2 do not agree exactly with those in Table 1 because of nonresponse to individual questions, and because some of the records required for validation of voter registration and voting were in litigation and thus not available.

The procedure for estimating the percentage of incorrect responses and sample size is somewhat different for the randomized response method. The sample size is estimated as 70 percent of those responding, since the remaining 30 percent answered a different question. The proportion of incorrect responses is estimated as the

Table 2. Proportion of Distorted Responses and Standard Errors

Methods	Threat				
	Voter Regis- tration	*Library Card*	*Bank- ruptcy*	*Vote Primary*	*Drunken Driving*
Face-to-Face	.15	.19	−.32	.39	−.47
	N = 92	N = 93	N = 38	N = 80	N = 30
	.037	.04	.075	.055	.09
Telephone	.17	.21	−.29	.31	−.46
	N = 89	N = 97	N = 41	N = 77	N = 68
	.039	.044	.075	.052	.073
Self-Administered	.12	.18	−.32	.36	−.54
	N = 80	N = 82	N = 31	N = 74	N = 28
	.036	.042	.083	.056	.094
Random Response[a]	.11	.26	.00	.48	−.35
	N = 61	N = 61	N = 26	N = 50	N = 23
	.058	.08	.00	.101	.141

[a]The standard errors for the random response method were computed using the formulation of Greenberg and others (1969).

difference between the total population estimate using validation data and the estimate obtained from using Formula 1. It is, of course, impossible to specify which respondents gave incorrect responses.

Table 2 is organized so that the threat dimension increases for most method conditions from low to high distortion. In all cases, except the random response-bankruptcy cell (.00), the proportions of distortion increase as threat increases. The threat dimension has been reordered, because the voter registration question was least distorting across all four methods. The library card question appeared to be more threatening than voter registration, at least as measured by proportion of distorted answers. Voting in the primary election had a higher rate of distortion than the bankruptcy question in all method conditions. (Some of this may have been due to errors in the list of primary voters.) The drunken driving question, with the exception of the random response cell, had the highest distortion rate.

As far as could be determined, there were no incorrect responses in the direction opposite to the expected one. Thus, we did not find persons who denied owning library cards who actually had them or persons who claimed not to have voted who actually did vote in the primary election. Nor did we find any respondents in the general sample who reported being arrested for drunken driving.

Looking down the columns of Table 2, we find that the method treatment findings are not as clear-cut. Based on earlier research, one would expect to find the smallest effects for the most anonymous random response forms and the largest effects for the face-to-face methods. Another way of looking at the data is to note that response errors may be due either to overreporting of socially desirable acts, such as owning a library card, being registered to vote, or voting in a primary election, or underreporting of socially undesirable acts, such as being involved in a bankruptcy proceeding or being charged with drunken driving. Here the social interaction effects may yield different results. Overreporting of socially desirable acts might be highest for the more personal methods, whereas underreporting of socially undesirable acts might be highest for the more anonymous methods. The results in Table 2 weakly suggest this more complex hypothesis.

When the response error is an overreporting of a socially desirable act, the self-administered questionnaire is better than the other, more personal methods in seven of nine comparisons. When the response error is an underreporting of a socially undesirable act, the self-administered form is worse in five of six comparisons and equal on the other. Although the differences are small and not completely consistent, they tend to support the hypothesis.

The relation between personal interviewing and telephoning also bears on this issue. At low-threat levels, the distortion in the face-to-face interview is slightly lower than in telephone interviews. As the questions become more threatening, face-to-face interviews have more errors than telephone interviews. This result weakly supports Hyman's theory (1954) that the degree of social involvement or "physical presence" of the interviewer can contribute to response distortion. When the interviewer is removed to a telephoning situation and the questions become more personal, the physical absence of the interviewer tends to reduce social involvement, and results from telephoning are less distorted than personal interviewing.

The random response model tended to produce higher variances across threat treatments. The results ranged from zero distortion in the bankruptcy cell to .48 in the voting cell. In the highest threat condition, random response yielded the lowest rate of distortion. However, in the March primary voting question, the model yielded the greatest distortion. In a somewhat threatening bankruptcy question, the distortion was zero.

The bankruptcy variable is unique, in that part of the sample might not have perceived the question as threatening but rather as an opportunity to tell of a shrewd business maneuver. This point causes difficulty in evaluating the raw proportions. However, in the drunken driving condition, the model was the lowest in response bias. Initially, as one looks across the treatments, it is difficult to evaluate the model's performance in total. The random response technique did not, however, remove *all* error from the responses.

It is evident that random response procedures are least effective in reducing overreporting of socially desirable acts. If anything, they are even worse than responses to direct questions. (The randomized response questions were, of course, asked in the context of a face-to-face interview.) Self-administered and telephone interviews work best on reducing overstatements. The same results were found by Weiss (1968). Randomized response procedures were, however, most effective in reducing underreporting of socially undesirable acts, whereas self-administered forms were the least effective.

To test the statistical significance of the results in Table 2, an analysis of variance was made on the raw data. Table 3 presents the results of these computations. It can be seen that the threat treatment was significant at the .01 level. The method effect, however, was not significant. With only one observation per cell, it is impossible to determine within-cell variance. Kirk (1968, p. 227) outlines a procedure for handling ANOVA with $N = 1$ based on Tukey's (1949) test procedure for a factorial design experiment. If Tukey's F-test for nonadditivity is insignificant, the interaction term can be used to test the treatment effects. The interaction of the data for this study was not significant. The data were also transformed using an arcsine transformation. An analysis of variance on the transformed data again found the method effect not significant and the threat effect significant at the .01 level.

In addition to the results in Table 2, one might make other observations about this random response model, which is a relatively new technique. Generally, the model was well received by both interviewer and respondent. During the course of the interview, only 5 percent of the sample who used the random response model said it was confusing, silly, or unnecessary.

The interviewers were asked to evaluate each respondent's reaction to the random response box. Table 4 shows the results of each question by sample type. The general sample and the bank-

Table 3. Analysis of Variance of Proportional Data

Source	Sum of Squares	Degrees of Freedom	Mean Square	F Ratio
Treatment A (Method)	.76	3	.25	.446
Treatment B (Threat)	17.45	4	4.36	7.79[a]
Residual	6.67	12	.56	

[a]Significant at .01 level.

Table 4. Percentage of Interviewers' Answers to Questions About the Random Response Model

Answer	General Sample	Bankrupts	Drunken Drivers
Think the Respondent Understood Use of the Random Response Box	90.0	89.2	78.4
Think the Respondent Accepted Explanation of the Box and Believed That His or Her Answers Really Were Private	92.2	89.2	78.4
N	90	37	37

rupts appear to follow the same distribution. However, the percentages of "yes" responses for the drunken drivers drop off somewhat.

Chronic anxiety was significantly related to response distortion for personal interviewing and self-administration but not for telephoning. Across anxiety levels, the telephone method appeared to be more stable than the other methods.

One of the principal reasons for taking acute anxiety measures was to validate the threat dimension. Generally, the dimension was validated with library card and voting behavior at the low end and court and traffic questions at the high end. Response distortions were significantly different between the high- and low-acute groups. The acute effect was significant at the .05 level, but method of administration proved to be insignificant. There were significant differences between the high- and medium-acute groups with personal interviewing and between the high and low groups with self-administered forms. Telephoning did not show any significant differences among the acute-anxiety groups. The distortion rate for the telephone method was also the lowest across acute groups. The random response model produced acute-anxiety scores that were generally close to or higher than those for personal interviewing. Further discussion of these relations is found in Chapter Five.

Conclusions

It is clear from this experiment that no data collection method is superior to all other methods for all types of threatening questions. If one accepts the results at face value, each of the data-

gathering methods is best under certain condi'
domized response procedure gives the lowest disto'
ing questions about the performance of socially undes..
obvious, however, that one does not always obtain unbiased a..
using random response models. The 35 percent understatement or
drunken driving is still a major response bias, although it is lower
than for other methods. The use of randomized response procedures requires very large samples for any multivariate analysis of
the relation between the threatening question and independent
variables. For many uses, the loss of information from randomized
response would not be compensated by a modest reduction in response bias. Self-administered procedures are slightly better than
other methods for reducing overstatements on questions about performance of socially desirable acts but are worse on questions about
undesirable acts. In addition, the cooperation rate is lowest for
self-administered questionnaires. There do not appear to be any
meaningful differences in response bias between telephone and
face-to-face interviews, except that, for this large-city sample, cooperation was highest by telephone. This study again indicates the
usefulness of telephone procedures, especially in metropolitan
areas. Ultimately, this study suggests that highly threatening questions have high response biases that are not generally affected by the
way in which the question is asked, even if privacy is preserved.

Chapter Two

Impact of Question Structure and Length

Empirical evidence shows that the impact of question threat is mediated by several variables, particularly question structure and question length. In *Response Effects in Surveys* (1974), we arrived at the following conclusions about these variables and question threat: (1) Question structure and question length do not affect response effects for nonthreatening questions. (2) For threatening questions, closed-ended questions elicit negative response effects (underreporting), perhaps because closed endings increase question threat by forcing the respondent to choose from a number of alternatives.

Note: Adapted from Edward Blair, Seymour Sudman, Norman M. Bradburn, and Carol Stocking, "How to Ask Questions About Drinking and Sex: Response Effects in Measuring Consumer Behavior," *Journal of Marketing Research*, August 1977, *14*, 316–321.

Closed-ended questions also seem to be more sensitive to social desirability factors and to result in depressed reporting about socially sensitive behavior or attitudes. Open-ended questions thus seem most appropriate for threatening topics. (3) Response effects for threatening items decrease with increasing question length, and thus longer questions (exceeding thirty words) may be most appropriate for threatening topics. Since these conclusions were derived from several very specific studies, large-scale investigation of question structure, question length, and response effects was needed to confirm these effects and to explore their interactions. This chapter reports on a large-scale investigation of these factors, and a new variable, wording familiarity, is also explored.

Our literature review suggested that response effects for threatening items increase sharply with increasing average word length, a common surrogate for wording difficulty. Because standard questions that use simple, easy-to-understand words minimize response effects from this source, efforts to reduce wording difficulty led to the idea of asking respondents for their own words, particularly where standard words were not common words. Familiar words may, in addition, relax the respondent and thus improve reporting even beyond the effect of difficulty reduction. However, familiar words may also have threatening effects that damage reporting, particularly when a closed-form response card presents street-language variations of a standard word. This study tentatively hypothesized that increasing familiarity should have effects similar to decreasing difficulty.

Hypotheses

This study investigated three hypotheses, which we call H_1, H_2, and H_3.

- H_1: Open-ended questions elicit higher levels of reporting for threatening behavioral topics than closed-ended questions. (Threatening behavioral topics invariably elicit underreporting; thus, higher reporting levels can be interpreted as a reduction in negative response effect rather than an increase in positive response effect. This point is substantiated in the later section on validation of results.)
- H_2: Long questions (containing more than thirty words) elicit

higher reporting levels for threatening behavioral topics than short questions.

• H_3: Familiar questions (defined in this study as questions that use wording chosen by the respondent) elicit higher reporting levels for threatening behavioral topics than questions employing standard researcher-chosen wordings.

Design of the Study

A national sample of 1,200 adults (over eighteen years of age) was drawn from the National Opinion Research Center's (NORC) national master sample; probability sampling with quotas was used. In each of the fifty areas that fell into the sample, the best interviewer then available to NORC was used to ensure maximum data quality. Interviewers who agreed to participate completed a practice case, and employment for the study was contingent on a high-quality practice interview. A total of 1,172 personal interviews was obtained for final analysis.

The same base questionnaire was used in all 1,172 cases. The most effective version of those questions is given in Appendix B. After answering questions about various leisure and sports activities and about general happiness and well-being, respondents were asked questions on threatening topics in the following order: gambling, social activities, drinking alcohol, getting drunk, using marijuana, using stimulants and depressants, sexual activity, and demographic items including income. Gambling, drinking, getting drunk, smoking marijuana, using stimulants and depressants, and sexual activity (petting or kissing, intercourse, and masturbation) were thought to be threatening topics of serially increasing threat. Placing these items in invariant order of increasing threat was considered necessary to minimize breakoffs and refusals. The fixed order was also justified by our earlier conclusions that order effects were minor in causing response effects and that increasing interviewer-respondent rapport should depress negative response effects on later items (thus promising a conservative test of the hypothesized negative response effects). DeLamater and MacCorquodale (1975) offer more recent evidence that question order has little effect on response effects for sexual-behavior questions.

Results from a final question asking whether various questionnaire sections would make most people very uneasy, moderately uneasy, slightly uneasy, or not at all uneasy show the presumed threat order to be correct. Table 5 presents some of these results. All the sections are properly ordered, and the only departure from order within sections is for the drug items. Marijuana use was viewed as a more threatening topic than stimulant or depressant use, probably because more people use marijuana.

Hypothesis testing involved a 2 × 2 × 2 factorial manipulation of threatening items on the base questionnaire. Open-ended versus closed-ended questions constituted a question-structure manipulation. The closed-ended and open-ended questions were identical, except for the provision of response categories in the closed-ended questions. Long versus short questions constituted a question-length manipulation. The long and short questions were identical, except for the use of at least fifteen prefatory words in the long questions. Familiar versus standard wording constituted the final manipulation, question wording. The familiar and standard wordings were identical, except that, for the familiar wordings, the interviewer asked the respondent to suggest the wording to be used. The 2 × 2 × 2 design resulted in eight distinct questionnaires, each

Table 5. Percentage of Respondents Who Feel Most People Would Be Very Uneasy or Not at All Uneasy About Topic

Topic	Very Uneasy	Not at All Uneasy
Masturbation	56.4	11.8
Marijuana	42.0	19.8
Intercourse	41.5	14.5
Stimulants and Depressants	31.3	20.2
Intoxication	29.0	20.6
Petting and Kissing	19.7	26.3
Income	12.5	32.7
Gambling with Friends	10.5	39.7
Drinking	10.3	38.0
General Leisure	2.4	80.8
Sports Activity	1.3	90.1

Note: N = 1,172, but actual N varies slightly from question to question because of no answers.

using one combination of factor levels throughout all threatening items.

The question manipulations are best illustrated by an actual example. The questionnaire contained an item asking how many times in the past year respondents had become intoxicated. In the closed, short, standard questionnaire form (the form expected to obtain the poorest reporting), this item read: "In the past year, how often did you become intoxicated while drinking any kind of beverage?" Respondents were handed a card listing these response categories:

Never	Every few weeks
Once a year or less	Once a week
Every few months	Several times a week
Once a month	Daily

In the open, long, familiar form (the form expected to obtain the best reporting), the respondents first provided their own word for intoxication through the following item: "Sometimes people drink a little too much beer, wine, or whiskey so that they act different from usual. What word do you think we should use to describe people when they get that way, so that you will know what we mean and feel comfortable talking about it?" The intoxication item then read: "Occasionally, people drink on an empty stomach or drink a little too much and become (respondent's word). In the past year, how often have you become (respondent's word) while drinking any kind of alcoholic beverage?" No response categories were offered for either item.

Each respondent answered one of the eight questionnaires. Each geographic segment sampled in the study contained eight cases, so that every form of the questionnaire was used once in every segment. The starting form was randomized across segments to avoid sequence effects (such as interviewer practice effects). Because interviewers typically did three segments each, they used each form three times.

Results

The results indicated that threatening items must be separated into two categories—items that ask about performing a behavior even once within some time span and require "yes" or "no" responses and items that ask about the frequency or intensity (how often or how much) of a behavior and require some qualified answer. Questions requiring "yes" or "no" responses showed no systematic interpretable effects from the question-length and wording-familiarity manipulations (question structure was not amenable to manipulation for these items). Questions requiring qualified answers proved consistently sensitive to the question-structure, question-length, and wording-familiarity manipulations. Nonthreatening items elicited virtually flat reporting across questionnaire manipulations.

Table 6 shows the stability of yes-or-no responses across question forms. The percentages of respondents answering "yes" to the gambling items show ranges of less than six percentage points and thus indicate little variation by question length in reporting. The percentages of respondents answering "yes" to the drinking and sexual-activity items show similarly low ranges of less than seven points. Almost none of these differences is statistically significant, and their shifting directionality suggests that none of them is practically significant. This stability of reporting indicates that question length and wording familiarity do not influence respondents' willingness to report having performed sensitive behaviors at least once. The decision to report any behavior always precedes the decision of how much behavior to report, even if the yes-and-no question is not asked explicitly. Apparently, respondents are not influenced systematically by question length and by wording familiarity in making that first decision.

Table 7 indicates that the second decision, how much to report, is much more sensitive to question-format manipulations. Long, open-ended questions were hypothesized to be the best format for asking threatening items. All the Table 7 breakdowns show that long, open-ended questions, with familiar wording where relevant, obtained much higher levels of reporting than short, closed, standard questions. These consistent and sizable differences leave no doubt that open, long questions enhance reporting for threatening items asking "how much" or "how many." Even when the differences are tested on an item-by-item basis, all the differences between open-ended and closed-ended forms are statistically significant at

Table 6. Percentage of Respondents Answering "Yes" to Items, by Question Form

Question	Question Form		Long Question (N = 584)		Short Question (N = 588)	
	Long Question (N = 584)	Short Question (N = 588)	Familiar Wording (N = 298)	Standard Wording (N = 291)	Familiar Wording (N = 294)	Standard Wording (N = 294)
Gambling[a]						
Have you played cards for money in the past year?	29.2	30.3				
Have you bet on sports?	19.8	17.4				
Have you bet on elections?	6.9	12.4				
Have you been in a betting pool?	17.2	16.2				
Have you played dice games for money?	6.2	7.8				
Have you bought a state lottery ticket?	25.2	23.9				
Drinking[b]						
Have you ever drunk beer?			76.7		82.3	
Have you drunk beer in the past year?			59.8		65.8	
Have you ever drunk wine?			81.0		80.9	
Have you drunk wine in the past year?			64.8		62.5	
Have you ever drunk hard liquor?			79.8	82.5	85.7	81.0
Have you drunk hard liquor in the past year?			62.1	67.0	69.0	65.0
Sexual Activity[c]						
Have you engaged in petting or kissing in the past month?			75.6		76.2	
Have you engaged in petting or kissing in the past 24 hours?			42.9		36.6	
Have you engaged in intercourse in the past month?			67.9	66.1	69.4	69.2
Have you engaged in intercourse in the past 24 hours?			18.9	17.6	17.8	16.8
Have you masturbated in the past month?			10.9	11.1	10.9	7.0
Have you masturbated in the past 24 hours?			1.8	1.5	1.5	.4

[a]Question structure and wording familiarity were not manipulated for these items.
[b]Question structure was not manipulated for these items. Wording familiarity was manipulated only for the hard liquor questions.
[c]Question structure was not manipulated for these items. Wording familiarity was not manipulated for the petting and kissing items.

Table 7. Annual Means for Drinking and Sexual Activity Frequency Items, by Question Form

	Open-Closed Ended		Long-Short Question		Familiar-Standard Wording		Long, Open (Familiar)	Short, Closed (Standard)
Cans of Beer								
All Drinkers	301	173	267	204	a	a	320	131
	(437)	(476)	(438)	(475)			(208)	(246)
Drank in Past Year	300	186	257	229	a	a	286	147
	(356)	(368)	(342)	(482)			(167)	(186)
Glasses of Wine								
All Drinkers	97	57	92	61	a	a	116	45
	(453)	(475)	(463)	(465)			(222)	(234)
Drank in Past Year	95	68	94	69	a	a	108	55
	(361)	(377)	(375)	(363)			(179)	(181)
Drinks of Liquor								
All Drinkers	168	119	160	127	152	134	204	80
	(460)	(486)	(461)	(485)	(477)	(469)	(110)	(121)
Drank in Past Year	153	108	127	133	141	119	175	78
	(374)	(392)	(373)	(393)	(382)	(384)	(87)	(98)
Petting or Kissing[b]	223	196	220	198	a	a	232	184
	(405)	(430)	(417)	(418)			(206)	(219)
Intercourse[b]	124	107	123	108	116	112	137	91
	(348)	(369)	(352)	(365)	(364)	(353)	(93)	(100)
Masturbation[b]	102	49	82	58	77	63	182	49
	(43)	(61)	(56)	(48)	(58)	(46)	(11)	(14)

[a]Not manipulated.
[b]Question asked only of respondents who reported engaging in activity in past month.

the .05 level, and the differences between long and short forms are generally significant. Familiar wordings are not statistically superior to standard wordings when tested item by item, but the consistently good performance of the long, open-ended questions with familiar wordings suggests that they should be used unless inconvenient.

Table 7 presents two sets of results for drinking items. The first set includes only those respondents who had drunk the indicated beverage within the past year. The second set includes both these respondents and those who had drunk the beverage during their life but not in the past year. Respondents who had drunk at some time but not in the past year were significantly more sensitive to the length manipulation for both beer and liquor and were slightly more responsive to this manipulation for wine. The differential responsiveness is great enough on beer and liquor to turn nonsignificant effects for the past-year drinkers into significant effects for all drinkers. This differential effect supports the suggestion that longer questions improve reporting by giving the respondent more time to recall events.

Respondents were not asked the total number of drinks consumed annually. They were asked how many times a year they had drunk and how many drinks they had drunk on an average occasion. Categorical answers to the number of times each had drunk were converted to number of times per year, and these numbers were multiplied by number of drinks per time to form the data in Table 7.

Interaction among question structure, question length, and question wording in their impact on response effects has been an unexplored topic. The desire to evaluate interaction effects motivated the use of the factorial design in this study. Analysis of variance suggests that these factors do not interact. Only one first-order interaction is significant, and no second-order interactions reach significance. An isolated closure-by-length interaction for the masturbation-frequency item seems to have little pragmatic value.

The results of this study add to the understanding of response effects for threatening questions, although the three hypotheses receive only mixed support. Threatening items that ask about having performed a behavior even once and that require yes-or-no responses are insensitive to question-format manipulations. All three hypotheses must be rejected for these items.

Threatening items that ask about frequency or intensity of behavior and that require quantified answers are very sensitive to question structure and question length. H_1 and H_2 are supported for these items. H_3 must be rejected, although consistent results suggest the wisdom of using familiar wordings. Also, interaction effects for these factors appear trivial.

Validation of Results

Although there are strong reasons to believe that increases in reporting are improvements in reporting for threatening behaviors, one would like direct proof. This study could not get validating evidence on an individual level. However, validating information is available on an aggregate level for the alcohol consumption items.

Because beer, wine, and liquor are taxed, aggregate consumption estimates are available on an annual basis. *Brewers Almanac 1975* (U.S. Brewers Association, 1975) lists taxed sales in gallons for 1974 and divides these figures by the estimated number of adults who are at least twenty-one years old to obtain per capita consumption of beer, wine, and liquor in 1974. Comparable figures can be developed from the reported data that cover drinking behavior between the summer of 1974 and the summer of 1975. These figures are per capita, so differences due to the different time frames should be trivial.

Table 8 presents the comparison of taxed consumption with

Table 8. Comparison of Estimates of Annual Reported Drinking by Question Form, and Taxed Sales

Beverage	Ounces of Reported Beverage Consumption per Person by Question Structure		U.S. Taxed Sales of Beverage in Ounces per Person[a]
	Long, Open-ended Question	Short, Closed-ended Question	
Beer	2,016	1,176	3,982
Wine	204	102	304
Hard Liquor	85	66	234

Note: The Ns for this data are given in Table 7.
[a]U.S. Brewers Association (1975).

reported consumption. Taxed gallon consumption for adults who are at least twenty-one years old is converted to ounce consumption for adults who are at least eighteen years old by application of the appropriate multipliers. Reported consumption is converted to the same base by assuming that a can of beer contains twelve ounces, a glass of wine three ounces, and a drink of liquor one ounce.

Reported beer, wine, and liquor consumption for the open, long form reaches only 51, 67, and 36 percent of the taxed sales figures, respectively. Wine is better reported than beer or liquor, because more beer and liquor consumption occurs outside the home, where it is subject to greater underreporting. The fact that substantial underreporting remains even at the higher level indicates that increased reporting is improved reporting, not positively biased reporting. It is evident that improved forms do not completely solve problems of underreporting due to threat, although they help.

Table 9 offers further comparisons with this study's results. Louis Harris (1974) reports a study for the National Institute on Alcohol Abuse and Alcoholism that contained drinking questions similar to the drinking questions in this study. Because Harris' reported results cannot be converted into a total consumption estimate, Table 9 presents comparisons based on frequencies of consumption. For all three items, the Harris results are about equal to or slightly higher than the results from the short, closed form. This outcome verifies the contention that short, closed-ended questions with standard wording provide reporting levels equal to those of other surveys and that these reporting levels can be improved

Table 9. Comparison of Estimates of Annual Reported Drinking Frequency, by Question Form, and Harris Drinking Frequency Estimates

Beverage	Long, Open-ended Question	Short, Closed-ended Question	Harris[a]
Beer	121.72	73.63	82.41
Wine	75.98	47.04	42.95
Hard Liquor	67.34	47.36	56.21

Note: The Ns for this data are given in Table 7.

[a]Harris (1974) includes only respondents who reported drinking in past month.

greatly by the use of long, open-ended questions with familiar wording.

A final validation is provided by the results of Chapter One, in which validation information was available for questions about having been convicted of traffic violations and about having gone through bankruptcy. The fact that reporting these events ranged from 27 percent to 75 percent across groups shows that negative response effects are persistent for threatening questions.

Chapter Three

Interviewer Variations in Asking Questions

Most of the literature on interviewer effects looks only at evidence of effects, such as between-interviewer variation, and not at the means by which those effects occur. It is clear, however, that interviewer effects occur through nonprogrammed interviewer behaviors—that is, through behaviors that originate with the interviewer rather than the researcher. For example, Hyman and others (1954) postulated that interviewer-expectation effects are actualized by means of probes, failures to probe, errors in recording, communication through feedback, or other, more subtle behaviors. Given the current interest in interviewer effects, this seems a good time to examine how often various nonprogrammed interviewer behaviors occur.

Note: Adapted from Edward A. Blair, "Nonprogrammed Speech Behaviors in a Household Survey," unpublished doctoral dissertation, Department of Business Administration, University of Illinois, 1978.

This chapter presents data showing both the frequencies and the effects of nonprogrammed speech behaviors in the nationwide study containing threatening questions described in Chapter Two. It also shows coders' abilities to recognize occurrences of those behaviors. The findings indicate that nonprogrammed behaviors occur on about one half of all question administrations, and that about 70 percent of the occurrences are likely to be recognized.

Among the more specific results is the finding that reading errors were the most common type of nonprogrammed speech behavior. One reading error occurred for every two or three questions asked. For questions that were answered with amounts, rather than with a "yes" or "no," probing was about as common as reading errors. Otherwise, probing occurred less often than speech variations and nonprogrammed feedback. One variation and one feedback occurred for about every six questions asked. Some of these frequencies were mediated by question characteristics, respondent characteristics, or interviewer characteristics.

Design of the Study

The data were gathered, as noted, in the nationwide U.S. sample survey dealing with threatening topics described in Chapter Two. To minimize problems caused by interviewers and to get the cleanest possible test of the form effects, a select group of fifty-nine interviewers was used in this study. These interviewers were chosen as the best available in the areas surveyed, and their employment was contingent upon completion of an acceptable practice interview conducted with a friend or relative. Only female interviewers were used. The stringent selection process certainly produced a group of very good interviewers, and it may also have produced a group that was homogeneous and unusual in its frequencies of nonprogrammed speech behaviors. This possibility should be remembered in considering the data, although evidence against it is seen in the demographic similarity of these interviewers to other NORC interviewers, the fairly large variances in frequencies among these interviewers, and the data that show nonprogrammed behaviors increasing with years of interviewing experience.

Of the 1,172 interviews, 1,049 were tape recorded. The interviews not taped contained seventy-four refusals and forty-nine mechanical failures (either the recorder or the tape failed to work).

Data analysis showed that respondents who refused taping, respondents who did not refuse but were not taped, and respondents who were taped were virtually identical in their responses.

Of these taped interviews, 372 were coded for nonprogrammed speech behaviors. These 372 cases were selected from the first eight for each interviewer that were taped and that met standards of completeness and sound quality. Each was coded by two different coders so that two points of view were available on each case. The full data were used for estimating coding reliabilities and probabilities of recognizing behavioral occurrences. To get an estimate of the frequencies of recognizable behaviors, however, only one coder's ratings were selected. This selection process systematically assigned every other question of a case to each of the two coders for that case and employed rotation across cases to ensure balanced representation of coders on questions. The selection procedure was used to reduce the amount of data manipulated and was justified by the logic that a respondent does not get a second opinion on what the interviewer did. Thus, the frequencies reported in this chapter are based on 41,292 question administrations (111 each in 372 interviews) coded by two people. The reliabilities and recognition data are based on over 80,000 records.

Frequency of Occurrence

This section discusses data on some types of behaviors that were collapsed out of a list of fifty-seven behaviors coded. The interviewer behaviors considered are reading errors, speech variations, probes, and feedback. Reading errors include adding or omitting words or phrases and substituting words. Variations include false starts, word reorderings, word repetitions, corrected substitutions, and stuttering or coughing. The respondent behaviors considered are laughter or comments about the question or behaviors that require the interviewer to probe, such as requests for clarification or inappropriate responses.

Some important types of interviewer behaviors are not shown in the tables, because they occurred infrequently. Leading probes occurred about once in every hundred questions, and skip errors and misrecorded answers occurred even less often. Table 10 shows frequencies for the remaining interviewer behaviors and breaks

Table 10. Average Number of Speech Behaviors per Question by Interviewer Characteristics

Interviewer Characteristics	Reading Errors	Speech Variations	Probes	Feedback	N
All Interviewers	.293	.116	.140	.161	59
Standard Deviations	(.145)	(.063)	(.069)	(.155)	
Range	.021–.652	.040–3.78	.011–.402	.001–1.007	
Race					
White	.296	.110	.140	.170	51
Black	.276	.151	.151	.107	9
Age					
Under 40	.238	.101	.114	.148	16
40–49	.323	.102	.128	.133	18
50 and Over	.307	.136	.165	.190	25
Education					
No College	.298	.129	.156	.168	26
Some College	.290	.098	.132	.115	15
Graduated from College	.288	.112	.124	.190	18
Experience					
Under 1 Year	.260	.067	.097	.103	8
1–5 Years	.276	.117	.146	.161	33
Over 5 Years	.339	.135	.149	.186	18

down these frequencies by interviewer race, age, education, and experience. The numbers shown in Table 10 are average numbers of behaviors per question asked—that is, total behaviors divided by total questions. The first line of Table 10 indicates that roughly three errors occurred in the reading of every ten questions. About one-and-one-half probes and feedbacks each occurred in the same span. The second line gives the standard deviations of behaviors across interviewers, and the third line gives the lowest and highest individual interviewer averages. The standard deviations are large relative to the means, indicating considerable variance among interviewers. This is most apparent for feedback to the respondent, where a 1.007 outlier creates some difficulties in interpreting averages and variances.

Given the large variance among interviewers, it is not surprising that no significant differences in frequencies of behaviors can be attributed to the background characteristics of the interviewers. However, some nonsignificant differences do exist. The most interesting of these are the comparisons that show all types of behaviors increasing with interviewer experience. Older interviewers (over fifty) also show higher levels of all behaviors. It appears that older, more experienced interviewers are less formal in their behavior and less likely to present a standardized measurement instrument to the respondent.

Table 11 presents the same four interviewer behaviors broken down by respondent characteristics. This table also shows respondent laughter or comments, as well as behaviors that require the interviewer to probe. The overall means are somewhat different from those given in Table 10, because Table 10 included all questions, but Table 11 is based on a reduced set of items of key interest. Sex, race, and age are considered in Table 11, because these characteristics would generally be apparent to the interviewer. Sex and race had no impact on behavior frequencies, but the differences across age groups are interesting. Interviewer behaviors such as reading errors, probes, feedback, and respondent behaviors such as requests for clarification or inappropriate answers all increased as respondent age increased. The effects for probes and respondent behaviors, which are interrelated, are significant. These results confirm the image of elderly respondents who like to interact with the interviewer and often need prompting to be kept on track.

Table 11. Average Number of Speech Behaviors per Question by Respondent Characteristics

Respondent Characteristics	Reading Errors	Speech Variations	Probes	Feedback to R	R's Comments About the Question	Other Salient Behavior by R	N
All Respondents	.335	.159	.157	.163	.078	.161	372
Standard Deviations	(.045)	(.027)	(.028)	(.048)	(.021)	(.033)	
Sex							
Male	.328	.157	.151	.178	.056	.153	174
Female	.341	.163	.163	.150	.097	.168	197
Race							
White	.336	.159	.154	.165	.078	.157	287
Black	.304	.159	.168	.151	.082	.181	70
Age							
18–34	.299	.146	.097[a]	.137	.073	.119[a]	144
35–64	.349	.175	.179	.176	.089	.173	169
65 and Over	.374	.153	.246	.198	.074	.226	55

Table 12 examines the effects of the task on the occurrence of these behaviors and shows the average numbers of speech behaviors per question broken down by the three question-format manipulations used in this study. Only questions that were manipulated are included in Table 12 to ensure comparability across formats. As this table shows, the only apparent effect of question form on speech behaviors is the impact of question length on the numbers of reading errors and speech variations. Errors and variations increase as the opportunities for them increase. The difference between open and closed forms in the amount of feedback given is not readily explainable. However, there is an interesting difference related to the open and closed forms. The values for probes, feedback, and respondents' comments and behaviors do not vary within form manipulations but seem to be inconsistent across manipulations. The larger values for the open and closed column occur because items with yes-and-no response alternatives were not included in these columns, and yes-no questions elicit less interchange between the interviewer and respondent. Two task variables not considered in Table 12 are question threat and interview sequence (that is, how many interviews the interviewer has done on the study as of this interview). Analyses of these variables are presented in later sections.

Some of the frequencies from this study can be compared with data obtained by Cannell, Lawson, and Hausser (1975), and the differences are small. For this study, probing was about 24 percent as common as question asking for questions other than those with yes-and-no responses; Cannell found 23 percent. Leading probes were 7 percent as common as acceptable probes on this study versus 11 percent in Cannell's research. Also, Cannell found that nonprogrammed feedback is, overall, more common than probing, as did this study.

Together, Tables 10, 11, and 12 provide some interesting insights into the possibilities of having interviewer effects communicated through various speech channels, but they do not tell the whole story. The occurrence of a behavior is not sufficient cause for an effect. That behavior must be noticed. Estimates of the proportion of interviewer speech behavior that is noticed can be derived from the interpenetrating nature of coder assignments. For each pair of coders and each such behavior, we calculated how many

Table 12. Average Number of Speech Behaviors per Question by Form

Form	Reading Errors	Speech Variations	Probes	Feedback to R	R's Comments About the Question	Other Salient Behavior by R	N
Long	.335	.174	.092	.163	.075	.104	40
Short	.204	.085	.096	.141	.086	.094	40
Open	.256	.119	.248	.172	.141	.183	17
Closed	.278	.120	.233	.275	.112	.152	17
Familiar	.308	.131	.089	.146	.063	.067	22
Standard	.236	.123	.059	.125	.074	.080	22

Note: Data based on analysis of 372 interviews conducted by 59 interviewers.

times the two coders agreed that a behavior of interest had occurred and how many times each coder recorded a behavior that the other coder did not. Then, using the assumptions that all coding errors were errors of omission and that probabilities of recognition were independent across coders, it was a simple matter to estimate the total number of occurrences and in turn the number that had been missed by both coders. The assumptions used make it likely that probabilities of recognition are slightly understated; however, these assumptions are not unreasonable given the data.

The average probabilities of recognition were about .70 for all behaviors except feedback. Feedback was noticeably more difficult to recognize, as just over one half of feedbacks were estimated to have been coded. This difference is probably due to the ambiguous nature of most naturally occurring feedback. It is clear from these estimates that Tables 10, 11, and 12 omit some occurrences. Better estimates of frequencies of behaviors can be obtained by dividing frequencies of recognition given in these tables by the probabilities of recognition. Table 13 is an example of such adjusted estimates. To form Table 13, each column of Table 12 was divided by the average probability of recognition for that behavior. For example, all the Table 12 figures for reading errors have been divided by the .71 average probability of recognition for reading errors. This procedure assumes that probabilities of recognition do not vary across whatever is being compared (question formats in this table), and the data give no evidence of such variance for formats, interviewers, or respondent groups. The figures in Table 13 cannot be used in correlational or cross-tabular analyses, but they are better estimates of how often various behaviors occurred. One useful result of doing the adjustments is the attention drawn to feedbacks, which become more frequent relative to other behaviors, because they were not as well recognized.

Even with the upward adjustments, none of the nonprogrammed speech behaviors occurs in more than half of the question administrations. No more than three questions in ten have noticeable occurrences of any one behavior, and no more than five in ten have noticeable occurrences of any behavior. Furthermore, the random nature of noticing (probabilities of noticing were independent) argues against any meaningful communication pattern. This all

Table 13. Estimated "True" Number of Speech Behaviors per Question by Form

Form	Reading Errors	Speech Variations	Probes	Feedback to R	R's Comments About the Question	Other Salient Behavior by R	N
Long	.472	.242	.128	.313	.106	.151	40
Short	.287	.118	.133	.271	.121	.136	40
Open	.361	.165	.344	.331	.199	.265	17
Closed	.392	.167	.324	.529	.158	.220	17
Familiar	.434	.182	.124	.281	.089	.097	22
Standard	.332	.171	.082	.240	.104	.116	22
Average Probability of Recognition (Used as Divisor)	.71	.72	.72	.52	.69	.71	

Note: Data based on 372 interviews by 59 interviewers.

suggests that nonprogrammed interviewer speech behaviors are not a potent source of response effects in surveys.

Effects of Interviewer Behavior

The remaining sections of this chapter present data on the effects of nonprogrammed interviewer behavior. The next section considers two hypotheses about feedback—that giving feedback to respondents when they reported threatening behaviors would encourage them to report additional behaviors, and that interviewers would give less feedback as they gained more experience on the study and their administration of the questionnaire became routine. Neither of these hypotheses was supported by the data. The following section studies five hypotheses about extralinguistic anxiety cues. These cues were expected to correlate with interviewer anxiety during training for the study, with respondent uneasiness as measured by the uneasiness-rating item in the questionnaire, and with response distortions. Many of the analyses shown in this section have relationships in the hypothesized directions, but the relationships are too small to support any of the hypotheses significantly.

Effects of Feedback to Respondents. Cannell and various associates at the University of Michigan (U.S. National Center for Health Services Research, 1977) have found that giving favorable feedback to respondents after they report health symptoms encourages them to report additional symptoms. The first hypothesis of this study, then, was that respondents will answer "yes" to threatening-behavior questions more often when interviewers give positive feedback to "yes" answers.

Before discussing this hypothesis, it is useful to contrast this study with the circumstances in which Cannell and others have found feedback effects. The Michigan researchers have used programmed feedback throughout the interview; in the test cases, interviewers are trained to give feedback every time the respondent reports a health symptom. This feedback generally is either a positive reinforcement for having reported a symptom or a probe asking for further details about the symptom. No feedback at all is given when respondents report not having had a symptom. Through this procedure, respondents should receive a clear, consistent message that the interviewer wants the respondent to report symptoms and to do so in some detail.

This study did not program feedback. As a result, feedback was not uniformly administered. Each respondent was likely to have some reports of behaviors that received feedback and many that did not. Also, each respondent was likely to receive feedback for some reports of not having done behaviors. It seems likely that these inconsistencies in the administration of feedback dampened feedback effects. Further, the naturally occurring feedbacks encountered in this study were rarely as strongly worded as the reinforcements programmed by Cannell and others, and probing feedback was classified as probing rather than feedback. This last point is important, because the various Michigan studies have found somewhat spotty effects of reinforcement feedback on level of reporting and more consistent effects of probing feedback on quality of reporting. The first point is more important, because the positive feedback encountered in this study generally was so brief and weakly worded (for example, "good") that respondents may not have perceived it as reinforcement for their answers. In fact, most positive feedback so closely resembled neutral feedback that the two categories were combined to get enough observations for analysis.

Table 14 shows the tests of feedback results. In all the analyses, there is comparison of the subsequent answers of respondents who reported behaviors and received feedback and respondents who reported behaviors and did not receive feedback. Nonreporters are kept out of the no-feedback group to ensure a fair comparison, although this reduces the sample size considerably for some topics. Sample size for the feedback group is a problem throughout the analyses—items on marijuana, stimulants, and depressants do not appear in the table, and gambling items appear only in a cumulative form, because the number of people reporting these behaviors and receiving feedback is too small to analyze.

The first four rows in Table 14 consider whether feedback anywhere within a checklist series stimulates additional subsequent reporting. The questions on gambling are treated as a six-item checklist, although each was asked as a separate question. Respondents who received feedback reported less than those who did not on all four items. The next section of the table looks at pairs of questions separated by follow-up items concerning the first. Will feedback to an admission of having drunk beer encourage respondents to report having drunk wine, even though several questions about beer con-

Table 14. Percentage of Respondents Who Reported Threatening Behaviors After Receiving and Not Receiving Feedback to Reports of Other Behaviors

Items Given Feedback	Items Affected	Reporting With Feedback		Reporting Without Feedback	
Betting on Cards or Sports	Betting on Elections	0	(9)	20.9	(110)
Cards, Sports, or Elections	Betting on Pools	18.2	(22)	28.3	(120)
Cards, Sports, Elections, or Pools	Betting on Dice	13.8	(29)	14.0	(136)
Cards, Sports, Elections, Pools, or Dice	Betting on Lotteries	29.4	(34)	41.8	(134)
Report of Drinking Beer	Drinking Wine	89.2	(37)	89.1	(266)
Drinking Wine	Drinking Liquor	83.3	(36)	92.2	(268)
Petting or Kissing	Sexual Intercourse	87.5	(56)	80.7	(207)
Sexual Intercourse	Masturbation	12.5	(24)	12.7	(204)
Any Item About Beer	Report of Drinking Wine	88.6	(140)	89.6	(163)
Any Item About Wine	Drinking Liquor	89.8	(128)	92.1	(176)
Beer or Wine	Drinking Liquor	90.1	(192)	90.8	(141)
Petting or Kissing	Sexual Intercourse	83.0	(106)	81.5	(157)
Sexual Intercourse	Masturbation	12.3	(65)	12.9	(163)
Petting or Kissing or Sexual Intercourse	Masturbation	10.9	(119)	12.8	(149)

sumption are asked between the feedback and its effect? Will feedback to a report of drinking wine affect liquor reporting? According to Table 14, the answer in general is no. The data in Table 14 can also be used to examine whether feedback to items other than the admission of behaviors might also encourage reporting. The first line in the third section of the table tests whether feedback on any question in the beer series will affect reporting of having drunk wine. This includes questions about how often and how much beer was consumed (of course, the analysis is still limited to respondents who admitted drinking beer). Other rows in the third section consider similar effects, including effects lagged by one topic. This section, like the first two, shows no feedback effects; respondents who did receive feedback are more likely to report in only one of the six rows.

The data in Table 14 do not support the hypothesis of feedback effects in this study, and additional analyses not shown in the table are also nonsupportive. Feedback to the initial admission of behavior did not affect the reported frequency or amount of beer, wine, or liquor consumption, or the reported frequency of petting, intercourse, and masturbation. Also, no lagged effects appeared. Based on these results, we conclude that the first hypothesis is not supported.

That the first hypothesis was not supported makes the second hypothesis rather trivial. This hypothesis states that positive feedback to yes-answers will become less frequent and reporting of threatening behaviors will decline as the interviewer does more cases. If feedback has no effects, verifying this hypothesis merely establishes an interesting coincidence. However, we still tested the second hypothesis, because the weak nature of the feedback studied and its uncontrolled occurrence suggested that the first hypothesis might have failed because of method weaknesses. This analysis treated the correlations between interview sequence and number of feedbacks and between interview sequence and reporting for eleven key items in the questionnaire. Both series of correlations have averages under .02, with associated squared correlations around zero. These figures certainly do not support this hypothesis.

Causes and Effects of Extralinguistic Anxiety Cues. The last five hypotheses included in this chapter state that extralinguistic anxiety cues become more frequent with increasing tension in the interview, and that anxiety cues cause respondent uneasiness and response distortions. The presumed causal path is tension, causing cues that give rise to respondent uneasiness that in turn causes response distortion.

This section treats our test of the effects of anxiety cues before testing their cause — that is, before verifying that they really are anxiety cues. There are two reasons to do this. First, the effects of speech behaviors are the primary concern of this research. Thus, even if the behaviors cannot be verified as anxiety cues, we are interested in their effects. Second, the tests of whether anxiety cues do become more frequent with increasing tension are somewhat complicated. Three separate hypotheses are needed to investigate this relationship, and the tables that test these hypotheses require a fair amount of explanation. Before testing anything, however, we must specify what we mean by extralinguistic anxiety cues. Two types of speech behaviors are used as anxiety cues — speech variations that respondents can easily notice, and reading errors that might not be noticed. These behaviors were described earlier in this chapter.

We expected that speech variations and reading errors would cause increased respondent uneasiness by cueing respondents to interviewer uneasiness. Table 15 presents the results of the test of this hypothesis. For eleven items of critical interest, the percentages of respondents who said that most people would be uneasy about a topic are compared between cases where an error or variation occurred and cases where these cues did not occur. A quick glance at the bottom rows of the table shows that the average percentages are virtually identical, although large differences exist for some items, and that counts for a sign test are evenly split.

Two questions might be raised about Table 15. First, it might seem more appropriate to look at the total number of cues in entire sections of questions, since the sections are the basis for the uneasiness ratings. Second, it might be wiser to use the full distribution of uneasiness ratings and to compare mean uneasiness rather than the percentage of very uneasy respondents. These approaches would use more of the information available. However, these approaches would not fit previous findings about uneasiness effects as well as the

Table 15. Percentage of Very Uneasy Respondents[a] by Whether Error or Speech Variations Occurred

Item	Error		Speech Variations	
	No Occurrence	Occurrence	No Occurrence	Occurrence
Ever Drink Beer	10.44	7.94	11.29	2.00
Ever Drink Wine	10.39	7.69	9.27	14.89
Ever Drink Liquor	9.93	10.29	10.86	4.26
Intoxication Past Year	28.93	27.50	30.16	18.60
Ever Use Marijuana	40.13	46.00	39.87	47.92
Ever Use Stimulants	35.44	31.51	34.12	32.99
Ever Use Depressants	33.52	34.10	30.43	46.05
Petting Past Month	19.32	24.21	19.92	22.58
Intercourse Past Month	37.92	33.33	36.33	40.98
Masturbation Past Month	51.06	45.45	47.11	54.76
Income	9.66	13.73	11.85	9.59
Average	26.07	25.61	25.56	26.78
(Sign Counts)	(6)	(5)	(5)	(6)

[a] Respondents who said that questions about the topic would make *most people* very uneasy.

analyses shown in Table 15. Analyses of data from an earlier study indicated that uneasiness caused response distortion only for the lead items of question sections (see Chapter Five). Since response distortion is our ultimate interest, this finding suggests that it is best to use only the lead items, as Table 15 does. The same analyses also showed that response distortions were most severe among the very uneasy respondents. This finding argues for comparing the percentages of very uneasy respondents rather than mean anxiety. In any event, average uneasiness is highly correlated with the size of the very uneasy group, and the two are interchangeable in most analyses. On the whole, then, Table 15 seems to give a good test of the hypothesis. Averaging across items produces a reasonable summary of the table, since the differences between conditions do not appear to be correlated for related items. A less-powerful alternative is a sign test. Either summary shows that respondents are no more uneasy when anxiety cues occur than when cues do not occur.

If extralinguistic anxiety cues do not increase the percentage of very uneasy respondents, there is no obvious theoretical justification for expecting those cues to cause response distortions. Examination of the data does not show any such distortions. For example, the percentage of respondents who reported having engaged in the behavior in question was analyzed. Again, the percentages were averaged and counted to get summary measures, but these measures showed no effects from either reading errors or speech variations. Frequencies of behaviors, measured by the number of times per year, were also compared for the drinking and sexual-behavior items (the drug items are not used, because very few respondents were asked the frequency question). Again, the averages are close to each other, and the differences that do exist are in the wrong direction (response distortion would show up as lower reporting for these items). The hypothesis that anxiety cues cause response distortion is not supported.

The failure to find effects of speech variations and reading errors puts the tests of their cause in a new light. We can now question whether occurrences of these behaviors are correlated with other measures of tension in the interview. If they are, we will probably conclude that the respondent is exposed to noticeable cues about the interviewer's feelings of tension, but that respondents do not act upon these cues. If they are not, we will conclude that these behaviors do not affect respondent uneasiness and response distortion because they are not reliable indicators of tension, and that any influence the interviewer has on respondent uneasiness must proceed through other channels.

Three separate hypotheses present different points of view on whether anxiety cues become more frequent with increasing tension in the interview. The first hypothesis claims that the number of extralinguistic anxiety cues exhibited by interviewers increases as questions become more threatening. For example, more cues are expected when interviewers ask questions about sex than when they ask questions about drinking, which in turn would cause more reading errors and speech variation than questions about social activities. The next hypothesis states that interviewers who expect to have some difficulty in asking questions will exhibit more anxiety cues than interviewers who do not expect difficulty. The last hypothesis is that interviewers exhibit more anxiety cues when respondents are very uneasy than when respondents are not very uneasy. For example, respondents who feel that questions about gambling would make most people very uneasy should receive more anxiety cues when asked about gambling than respondents who feel that these questions would make most people moderately, slightly, or not at all uneasy. These three hypotheses are different points of view on the same relationship, because question threat, interviewer uneasiness, and respondent uneasiness all should serve as indicators of how much tension is in the air as a question is asked. They should be partially but not totally redundant—extralinguistic anxiety cues should be most frequent when an interviewer who expects difficulty asks a very uneasy respondent about the most threatening topic in the questionnaire.

Table 16 presents the results of the test of the first of the three hypotheses, that anxiety cues become more frequent as questions become more threatening. The topics in Table 16 are arrayed in order of threat according to the percentage of respondents who felt that questions about the topic would make most people very uneasy. Since some of the orderings are based on fairly small differences, the topics are also grouped into three levels of threat. Then, the average numbers of speech variations and the reading errors that occurred

Table 16. Average Number of Reading Errors and Speech Variations per Word Across Topics of Varying Threat

Topic	Percentage Very Uneasy[a]	Speech Variations per Word Topic Level	Reading Errors per Word Topic Level	Errors and Variations per Word	N
Television, Radio, and Record Use	2.43	.00315	.01508	.0182	3
Social Activities	3.29	.00487	.01293	.0178	5
Satisfaction with Life	3.57	.00361	.01528	.0189	6
Feelings of Well-Being	3.57	.00617	.01321	.0194	10
Frequency of Well-Being States	3.57	.00715	.01843	.0256	2
Gambling	8.88	.00410	.01039	.0145	6
Drinking	9.92	.00560	.01199	.0176	16
Income	11.57	.00733	.02366	.0310	1
Use of Stimulants or Depressants	34.08	.00721	.01689	.0241	2
Sexual Behavior	36.22[b]	.00684	.01004	.0169	6
Marijuana Use	41.18	.00586	.01666	.0225	6

Note: Data based on analysis of 372 interviews conducted by 59 interviewers.

[a] Percentage of respondents who felt that *most people* would be very uneasy about answering questions on the topic. The correlation between percentage uneasy and errors = .15, and the standard deviation of errors = .0043.

[b] Average of 20.44 percent for questions on petting or kissing, 37.36 percent for intercourse, and 50.85 percent for masturbation.

for every word in every question are compared across topics and levels. Cues per word are used rather than cues per question, because, as shown earlier, the length of the question affects the number of cues. (This will not be a problem in later tables, because comparisons will be made across administrations of the same questions.) The table shows a weak positive relationship between topic threat and frequency of anxiety cues. A breakdown between speech variations and reading errors shows that variations are the basis for the positive relationship. This finding is consistent with the results of the tests of cue effects, where variations had nonsignificant effects in the proper direction and errors had no effects.

Table 17 addresses the hypothesis that interviewers who expect more difficulty exhibit more anxiety cues. This table separates the interviewers according to their answers to a question about how difficult to ask they expected the survey as a whole to be. This question was asked in the self-administered questionnaire that interviewers completed during training for the study. On the average, interviewers who did not expect the questions to be easy made more reading errors than interviewers who expected the questions to be easy. However, these differences are far too small to be sig-

Table 17. Average Number of Reading Errors and Speech Variations per Question by Interviewers' Prior Expectations of How Hard to Ask the Survey Would Be

	Errors		Variations	
Item	Easy	Not Easy	Easy	Not Easy
Ever Drink Beer	.190	.207	.190	.132
Ever Drink Wine	.184	.144	.146	.126
Ever Drink Liquor	.215	.224	.133	.144
Intoxication Past Year	.139	.121	.127	.121
Ever Use Marijuana	.146	.207	.152	.167
Ever Use Stimulants	.525	.621	.392	.247
Ever Use Depressants	.772	.672	.323	.213
Petting Past Month	.278	.368	.266	.282
Intercourse Past Month	.177	.241	.171	.155
Masturbation Past Month	.038	.098	.127	.109
Income	.468	.690	.253	.213
Average	.285	.327	.207	.174
(Sign Counts)	(3)	(8)	(8)	(3)
N	158	174	158	174

nificant. The hypothesis that anxiety cues become more frequent with increasing expectations of difficulty is not supported.

Table 18 extends the analysis from speech variations and reading errors to probes and feedback, in an effort to see whether probes and feedback function as indicators of expected difficulty. The sign test for probing supports this hypothesis, but the overall results are inconclusive — probing increases, but feedback decreases with expectations of difficulty. Since we would expect both behaviors to move in the same direction, and since arguments can be made for either direction, it is difficult to come to any firm conclusion about the relation between interviewer expectations and behavior.

The last hypothesis states that more anxiety cues occur when respondents are very uneasy than when respondents are not very uneasy. Testing this hypothesis is quite simple. First, respondents who said that questions about some topics would make most people very uneasy are separated from respondents who said moderately, slightly, or not at all uneasy. Then, for topics where a reasonable number of respondents fell into the very uneasy group, the numbers

Table 18. Average Number of Probes and Feedback per Question by Prior Expectations of How Hard to Ask the Survey Would Be

	Probes		Feedback	
Item	Easy	Not Easy	Easy	Not Easy
Ever Drink Beer	.089	.109	.171	.149
Ever Drink Wine	.032	.057	.120	.138
Ever Drink Liquor	.038	.063	.146	.109
Intoxication Past Year	.089	.115	.222	.144
Ever Use Marijuana	0	.005	.095	.098
Ever Use Stimulants	.070	.144	.133	.098
Ever Use Depressants	.076	.098	.082	.115
Petting Past Month	.051	.109	.241	.201
Intercourse Past Month	.025	.040	.127	.121
Masturbation Past Month	.019	.029	.070	.121
Income	.481	.592	.399	.287
Average	.088	.124	.164	.144
(Sign Counts)	(0)	(11)	(7)	(4)
N	158	174	158	174

of anxiety cues each group received are compared. Table 19 shows the results of this comparison, summarized with the same unweighted averaging and sign tests we have been using throughout this section. The summaries clearly show that the hypothesis is not confirmed. Speech variations are almost exactly the same in the two groups. Reading errors are slightly more frequent when respondents are very uneasy, but the differences are small.

In a second effort to determine whether probes and feedback function as anxiety cues, we compared these behaviors between very uneasy and not very uneasy respondents. Table 20 shows the results.

Table 19. Average Number of Reading Errors and Speech Variations per Question by Respondent Uneasiness

	Errors		Variations	
Item	Not Very Uneasy	Very Uneasy	Not Very Uneasy	Very Uneasy
Ever Drink Beer	.108	.167	.168	.028
	(327)	(36)	(327)	(36)
Ever Drink Wine	.165	.111	.131	.222
	(327)	(36)	(327)	(36)
Ever Drink Liquor	.217	.194	.153	.056
	(327)	(36)	(327)	(36)
Intoxication Past Year	.124	.125	.144	.086
	(257)	(104)	(257)	(104)
Ever Use Marijuana	.153	.197	.138	.177
	(210)	(147)	(210)	(147)
Ever Use Stimulants	.581	.496	.338	.306
	(234)	(121)	(234)	(121)
Ever Use Depressants	.692	.702	.235	.339
	(234)	(121)	(234)	(121)
Petting Past Month	.299	.405	.291	.311
	(288)	(74)	(288)	(74)
Intercourse Past Month	.210	.184	.166	.199
	(228)	(136)	(228)	(136)
Masturbation Past Month	.069	.061	.109	.133
	(174)	(180)	(174)	(180)
Income	.595	.690	.243	.238
	(321)	(42)	(321)	(42)
Unweighted Average	.292	.303	.192	.191
(Sign Counts)	(5)	(6)	(5)	(6)

Table 20. Average Number of Probes and Feedback per Question
         by Respondent Uneasiness

	Probes		Feedback	
Item	Not Very Uneasy	Very Uneasy	Not Very Uneasy	Very Uneasy
Ever Drink Beer	.085	.167	.135	.333
	(327)	(36)	(327)	(36)
Ever Drink Wine	.052	.028	.132	.167
	(327)	(36)	(327)	(36)
Ever Drink Liquor	.049	.056	.113	.167
	(327)	(36)	(327)	(36)
Intoxication Past Year	.117	.058	.222	.115
	(257)	(104)	(257)	(104)
Ever Use Marijuana	.005	0	.129	.068
	(210)	(147)	(210)	(147)
Ever Use Stimulants	.103	.132	.115	.099
	(234)	(121)	(234)	(121)
Ever Use Depressants	.102	.083	.107	.074
	(234)	(121)	(234)	(121)
Petting Past Month	.077	.095	.239	.230
	(288)	(74)	(288)	(74)
Intercourse Past Month	.030	.029	.092	.162
	(228)	(136)	(228)	(136)
Masturbation Past Month	.012	.017	.052	.139
	(174)	(180)	(174)	(180)
Income	.523	.690	.355	.333
	(321)	(42)	(321)	(42)
Unweighted Average	.105	.123	.154	.172
(Sign Counts)	(5)	(6)	(6)	(5)

Unlike our previous attempt to use probes and feedback, this time we find consistent differences—the very uneasy respondents receive more probes and more feedback. It is difficult, however, to interpret this finding, since we have not established a theoretical framework to guide our judgment. The most reasonable conclusion might be that probes and feedback are a response to uneasiness rather than a cause of it. Very uneasy respondents may give tentative, ambiguous responses in an effort to gauge the interviewer's feelings.

Cumulatively, then, the data refute the belief that speech variations and reading errors become more frequent as the interview becomes more tense. This finding is useful in light of the knowledge that these behaviors did not cause increased respondent uneasiness or response distortion. It suggests that speech variations and reading errors are not always indicators of uneasiness, but that, perhaps more often, they are simply speech variations and reading errors. As a result, counting speech variations and reading errors does not provide a reliable measure of interview tension, and respondents do not react to every variation or error.

This is not to say that the tests of the last hypotheses are totally unencouraging. What differences do occur are frequently in the hypothesized directions—so frequently, in fact, as to be tantalizing. One is struck by a feeling that the difficulty of accurately measuring what is happening handicaps the ability to test relationships. This difficulty will affect all efforts to investigate the effects of extralinguistic anxiety cues and must be overcome before we can hope for conclusive research on the subject.

Conclusions

Nonprogrammed interviewer speech behaviors occurred in over one half of the questions asked. Over one third of the questions were not read exactly as written. This confirms many researchers' belief that the survey presents a nonstandardized stimulus to the respondent. The only respondent characteristic that influenced the frequency of nonprogrammed speech behaviors was age. Older respondents gave more inappropriate responses and asked more often for clarification. In turn, interviewers probed older respondents more frequently.

Nonprogrammed speech behaviors increased (although not significantly) with interviewer experience. More-experienced interviewers made more reading errors, engaged in more variations, probed more often, and gave more feedback. This finding may reflect a less-formal approach to interviewing by practiced interviewers.

Respondents' answers elicited feedback more frequently than they elicited probes, except for questions that required quantified responses. Once one accepts the somewhat surprising frequency of feedback, this finding makes sense—there is not much to probe in a yes-no answer or an answer from a four-point scale.

Speech variations and reading errors increased as questions became longer and there were more linguistic events to stumble over. Feedback to reports of threatening behaviors did not significantly encourage reporting of additional threatening behaviors. Speech variations and reading errors did not increase with interview tension and did not cause respondent uneasiness or response distortion. Interviewer's expectations appear to have no effort on their nonprogrammed speech behaviors.

What do these data mean? First, they may mean that all the interesting facts about the occurrence of nonprogrammed speech behaviors are not relevant to the validity of survey data. The behaviors occur, but they do not affect the data. Second, they may mean that a different method is needed to capture the effects of these behaviors.

We leave this study with mixed emotions. It speaks well for the validity of survey measurement that many interviewer behaviors do not have demonstrable effects. However, we might wish just a little that we could have found effects, especially for the anxiety cues. We know that respondent uneasiness does occur and that it causes response distortions. Locating an external cause for this uneasiness would have given us an opportunity to control it through interviewer training. Now, we must look to future research to solve our problems.

Chapter Four

Role of Interviewer Expectations

In the last chapter, we failed to find any systematic relation between the interviewers' expectations about the difficulty of the interview and their nonprogrammed speech behaviors. In this chapter, we investigate interviewer expectations further, this time in relation to the respondents' answers to the questions in the interview schedule. Interviewers' expectations might cause response effects in several ways. The interviewer may communicate his or her expectations to the respondents, who may then try to fulfill these expectations. The interviewer may lead respondents with probes or may fail to probe unclear or inappropriate answers and try to record what the respondent meant to say. Also, the interviewer may incorrectly

Note: The original version of this article appeared under the title "Modest Expectations: The Effects of Interviewers' Prior Expectations on Responses," by Seymour Sudman, Norman M. Bradburn, Edward Blair, and Carol Stocking, published in *Sociological Methods and Research*, November 1977, *6*, 177–182, and is reprinted here with the permission of the publisher, Sage Publications, Inc.

record answers without asking the questions. The extent of expectation effects is not well understood. This chapter reports some analyses of interviewers' expectations and response variation.

Expectations about a study may be formed before or after entering the field (prior and situational expectations). Prior expectations may relate to means and distributions of results. Hyman and others (1954) describe "probability expectations," in which the interviewer anticipates a certain distribution of responses and presumably tries to fulfill that distribution. Rosenthal (1966) has studied hypothesis fulfillment in psychological experiments where prior expectations about differences in the mean scores of subject groups somehow are fulfilled.

Prior expectations may also relate to anticipated difficulty in asking the questions of the survey, to respondent uneasiness about answering the questions, or to data-quality variables such as levels of overreporting or underreporting and percentages of no-answer responses. Presumably, interviewers who anticipate difficulty with a study or high item nonresponse will be less aggressive about pursuing vague, evasive, or improbable responses or will communicate a lack of self-confidence to the respondent.

Question-sensitivity and data-quality expectations can also arise within the interview. Hyman and others (1954) distinguish two types of situational expectation—role expectation and attitude-structure expectation. Role expectation arises from identification of the respondent with some social role. For example, the interviewer might typecast a well-dressed respondent with a large house as a business executive and form concomitant expectations about that respondent's attitudes, behaviors, and socioeconomic characteristics. Attitude-structure expectation results from expectation of cognitive consistency; early responses generate expectations about responses for later items.

One would expect situational-expectation effects to be more powerful than prior-expectation effects. However, prior-expectation effects would be easier to detect. Situational effects would be distinguishable only with very careful monitoring of expectations and answers or with confederate respondents who varied their responses according to instruction. Prior-expectation effects would be revealed by between-interviewer variation.

Almost no research on prior expectations has ever been reported in the survey-methods literature, and almost no new results on situational expectations have been reported in the last twenty years. In our review of research into response effects, and in the results reported in the last chapter, we found that interviewer-related variables, including interviewers' expectations, are much less powerful than task variables, such as question threat, in causing response effects. This implies that interviewer-related variables should not receive high priority in investigations of response effects.

The most spectacular demonstrations of expectation effects almost surely contain inflated effects. Rosenthal's experimenter-expectation findings are laboratory based and are thus subject to the amplification effects that often occur in the laboratory as compared with the field. Smith and Hyman's (1950) demonstration of attitude-structure expectation effects used confederate respondents who presented extreme points of view with extreme consistency before giving a vague response. More naturalistic studies that measure interviewer variation without considering expectation, such as Hanson and Marks' (1958) study, show 5 percent or less of total response variance as attributable to interviewer variation. But this does not mean that expectation effects should be ignored. Interviewers do seem to contribute some small amount of variance to survey results, and studies of expectation do show effects, even if inflated. This chapter contains data from a study that estimated interviewer effects in addition to some larger sources of response effects. One important variable in the study was respondents' perceptions of social norms against discussing topics. In an effort to see how much of this social uneasiness was interviewer-related, we obtained interviewer expectations of general-study difficulty, specific-question difficulty, and respondent uneasiness. We also obtained expectations of overreporting or underreporting levels and of no-answer rates. This information allowed us to separate prior-expectation effects from total interviewer-related variance.

Design of the Study

The results are from the national U.S. sample survey of 1,172 respondents described in Chapter Two and discussed in the last chapter. Interviewer expectations were measured by a self-administered questionnaire that each interviewer completed after the training for this study but before any interviewing had been conducted. The questionnaire asked the following questions:

1. In general, how easy or difficult to ask do you expect this survey to be?
2. How difficult to ask do you expect each section to be?
3. How uneasy do you expect each section to make most respondents?
4. Which groups of people, if any, do you expect to feel at least moderately uneasy about answering the questions in each section?
5. About what proportion of respondents do you expect will not answer each section?
6. Do you expect the total results from each section to report less behavior than actually is done by the respondents, about the correct amount of behavior, or more behavior than actually is done?

Relative to the effects reported in Chapters One and Two, interviewer effects were expected to be small, but they were expected to be statistically significant and of practical importance except in two cases—for very threatening questions such as masturbation, where an overpowering social norm would swamp interviewer effects, and for very uncommon behaviors, such as stimulant and depressant use, where data would be too thin to show stable effects. The analysis of interviewer variation confirmed this expectation. No interaction effects between interviewers and question forms were expected, and none were observed.

Interviewer Contribution to Total Variance

Tables 21 and 22 present the first stage of analysis, the estimates of interviewer contribution to total variance. The major problem in interpreting these results is that interviewers were not randomly assigned to cases. Each interviewer worked within her home area, and typically only one interviewer worked an area. The total sample consisted of fifty-nine interviewers in fifty areas. Thus, it is not possible to separate area and interviewer effects. In Tables 21

Table 21. Percentage of Total Variance Due to Interviewer, Using SS_B/SS_T as a Measure

	Interview Location				
Item	Nonsouthern SMSA	Nonsouthern Non-SMSA	Southern SMSA	Southern Non-SMSA	Weighted Average
Gambling Scale	14	5	8	8	11
Income	11	4	4	4	8
Ever Smoke Marijuana	10	5	8	4	8
Intercourse Past Month	9	3	10	1	8
Petting or Kissing Past Month	9	3	7	2	7
Ever Drink Liquor	9	6	5	2	7
Ever Drink Wine	7	9	6	5	7
Ever Drink Beer	6	9	5	5	6
Ever Use Stimulants	6	1	6	6	6
Ever Use Depressants	7	5	3	1	6
Social Activities	6	6	2	7	6
Leisure Activities	7	1	4	4	5
Masturbation Past Month	6	3	6	2	5
How Often Intoxicated Past Year	6	7	4	2	5
Average	8	5	6	4	7
N Interviewers/N Respondents	37/634	7/164	10/212	5/126	

Table 22. Percentage of Total Variance Due to Interviewer, Using $\hat{\omega}^2$ as a Measure

| | Interview Location | | | | |
Item	Nonsouthern SMSA	Nonsouthern Non-SMSA	Southern SMSA	Southern Non-SMSA	Weighted Average
Gambling Scale	9	1	3	4	6
Income	6	0	0	1	4
Ever Smoke Marijuana	3	1	3	0	4
Intercourse Past Month	4	0	5	0	3
Petting and Kissing Past Month	4	0	3	0	3
Ever Drink Liquor	3	2	0	0	2
Ever Drink Wine	2	6	2	1	2
Ever Drink Beer	0	5	1	1	1
Ever Use Stimulants	1	0	1	3	1
Ever Use Depressants	2	1	0	0	1
Social Activities	1	2	0	3	1
Leisure Activities	2	0	0	1	1
Masturbation Past Month	0	0	1	0	0
How Often Intoxicated Past Year	0	2	0	0	0
Average	2	1	1	1	2
N Interviewers/N Respondents	37/634	7/164	10/212	5/126	

and 22, the most obvious location variables are controlled by presenting figures separately for nonsouthern Standard Metropolitan Statistical Areas (SMSAs), nonsouthern non-SMSAs, southern SMSAs, and southern non-SMSAs.

Table 21 shows that interviewers generally account for about 7 percent of the total response variance when the proportion explained is measured by the ratio of the sum of squares between interviewers to the total sum of squares. These figures have been controlled for respondent's education. Two other variables of interest, respondent's age and respondent's score on an abbreviation of a scale developed by Crowne and Marlowe (described in Chapter Six), were not controlled, because they did not vary across interviewers.

The proportion of variance explained by interviewers is generally stable across items and locations. Nonsouthern SMSAs have slightly higher proportions, which are probably due to a more heterogeneous group of interviewers and a slightly smaller average case load. The F-ratios associated with the figures in Table 22 show interviewer effects as large as or larger than those described by Hanson and Marks (1958) for demographic items.

Table 22 is presented because of a methodological weakness of the between-interviewer sum of squares to total sum of squares measure. The measure is simple to compute and has an intuitive meaning, but it is affected by changing the case load per interviewer. If the total sum of squares is roughly constant for a fixed number of respondents, one would increase the between-interviewer sum of squares, and thus the proportion of variance explained, by increasing the number of interviewers or reducing the case load. This problem can be corrected by using an analysis of variance analog to R^2 called $\hat{\omega}^2$, which adjusts for the number of treatment levels. The formula for $\hat{\omega}^2$ is:

$$\omega^2 = \frac{SS_B - (k-1)MS_{res}}{SS_T + MS_{res}}$$

where SS_B is the between-group (interviewer) sum of squares, k is the number of interviewers, MS_{res} is the mean square of the residual, and SS_T is the total sum of squares.

Of course, using ω^2 as a measure reduces the amount of variance attributable to interviewers. Table 22 shows figures that range around 2 percent. Although these percentages are small relative to question-form effects and actual differences in individual behavior, they are about as large as the combined effects of the two location variables.

Both of the measures used to form Tables 21 and 22 are legitimate indicators of the proportion of variance explained by interviewers. The ratio of between-to-total sums of squares is a more understandable measure; however, one must remember that it will change somewhat with a case load different from the twenty-case average used in this study. Both measures show small but generally significant interviewer effects on response variation. These interviewer effects may be caused by interviewer appearance, behavior, situational expectations, prior expectations, or some combination of these factors. Only a small proportion are attributable to prior expectations.

Expectations About General-Study Difficulty. Interviewers' expectations about the general difficulty of the interview appear to be weakly related to levels of reporting. Table 23 indicates that interviewers who anticipated difficulties with the questionnaire obtained lower percentages of respondents who reported ever engaging in activities than interviewers who thought the survey would be very easy. For the gambling, drinking, and sex items, interviewers who expected the interview to be very easy obtained levels of reporting 4 to 12 percent higher than interviewers who expected the interview to be difficult. These results seem unambiguous, but they are statistically significant only for beer drinking.

For some of the variables, the data do not show a linear trend. That is, although there is a difference between interviewers who think the interview will be very easy and those who think it will be difficult, the results in the middle bounce around. The small number of interviewers in each group accounts for the way the data bounce across columns. Combining interviewers who expected the study to be easy with those who expected it to be very easy would somewhat stabilize the data and would reduce the large differences on the sex items. The proportions of variance explained by interviewers' expectations of general difficulty range from 11 percent for beer down to 1 or 2 percent for most other items. Although these results do show some effect of prior expectations, other interviewer

Table 23. Response Related to Interviewer Expectations of General Difficulty

Item	Very Easy	Easy	Neither Easy nor Difficult	Difficult	Ratio of Very Easy to Difficult	R^2
Ever Drink Beer	86	84	76	73	1.18	.11
Ever Drink Liquor	90	83	82	78	1.15	.04
Ever Drink Wine	88	84	79	78	1.12	.02
Gambling Scale	1.17	1.08	1.03	.98	1.19	.02
Intoxication Past Year	36	29	33	28	1.29	.01
Petting and Kissing Past Month	81	75	80	71	1.14	.01
Intercourse Past Month	74	67	70	66	1.12	.01
Leisure Activities	4.46	4.43	4.50	4.19	1.06	.01
Social Activities	41.31	35.86	34.41	34.89	1.18	0
Ever Smoke Marijuana	21	20	21	22	.95	0
Income	$12,216	$13,531	$14,041	$11,747	1.04	0
N Interviewers/N Respondents	7/136	18/343	18/342	13/256		

Note: Numbers are percentage of respondents reporting this behavior, except for gambling scale, leisure, social activities, and income, where means are presented.

variables and what goes on in the interview are clearly far more important.

Cooperation rate proved to be unrelated to general-difficulty expectations of interviewers. Measures such as total doors approached, total refusals, and refusals from men and women did vary substantially by interviewer but were unrelated to interviewer expectations.

Expectations About Level of Reporting. Interviewers who expected their respondents to underreport behavior obtained lower levels of reporting, thus confirming the notion of the self-fulfilling prophecy. Table 24 shows that the interviewers who expected respondents to underreport obtained lower reporting on eight of thirteen items and higher reporting on three. The differences are smaller than those in Table 23, except for the item on income. A difference of $2,000 separates the average incomes reported to interviewers who expected income to be reported correctly or overreported and interviewers who expected income to be understated. The proportions of interviewer variance explained by interviewer expectations of overreporting or underreporting range from 6 percent for income down to 1 percent or less.

Expectations about level of reporting and about the general

Table 24. Response Related to Interviewer Expectations of Respondent Reporting Level

Item	Expect Correct or Overreporting	Expect Underreporting	Ratio	R^2
Income	$13,750 (764/39)[a]	$11,622 (247/17)	1.18	.06
Intercourse Past Month	69 (746/40)	67 (287/16)	1.03	.04
Intoxication Past Year	30 (462/23)	32 (644/33)	.94	.02
Gambling Scale	1.08 (846/43)	.93 (262/13)	1.16	.01
Petting and Kissing Past Month	78 (789/41)	71 (296/15)	1.10	.01
Ever Drink Beer	80 (742/37)	76 (374/19)	1.05	.01
Ever Drink Wine	82 (742/37)	78 (374/19)	1.05	0
Ever Drink Liquor	83 (742/37)	79 (374/19)	1.05	0

Note: Numbers are percentage of respondents reporting this behavior, except for income and gambling scale, where means are presented.

[a] Number of respondents/number of interviewers.

difficulty of the interview are correlated, but not highly. Correlations between the items measuring anticipated level of reporting and the item measuring general expected difficulty all have absolute values less than .26. These fairly small correlations would lead one to expect even sharper response effects when both expectations are combined. Table 25 shows this to be the case generally, with the proportions of explained variance slightly higher for most items.

Table 25 was formed by splitting the data into six groups. Expectations about whether the general interview will be easy, neither easy nor difficult, or difficult are cross-classified with expectations about whether the respondent will underreport. This table is a reminder of the small sample size that results when interviewers and not respondents are the independent observations. The final column is blank for the intercourse item, because no interviewers who expected the interview to be difficult also expected underreporting on this item. Splitting fifty-six interviewers six ways causes substantial sampling variability, and these results must be treated as suggestive rather than conclusive.

Other Expectations. Interviewer expectations also were measured for expected difficulty with each section of the interview, expected respondent uneasiness, specific groups of people expected to feel uneasy about sections of the interview, and anticipated proportion of respondents who would not answer various sections. These expectations had no additional impact on the data. Correlations between interviewers' expectations and respondents' actual uneasiness are near zero. Interviewer expectations about uneasiness appear to say something about the interviewer rather than about the respondent.

Expectations about proportion of respondents who will not answer are unrelated to actual no-answer rates, because variation between interviewers is just too small for effects to appear. No-answer responses are less than 1 percent of total responses for all items except intercourse, masturbation, and income, and are under 5 percent for those items.

Conclusions

The introduction of this chapter suggested that interviewers' prior expectations can affect survey data. For the behaviors reported in this study, it is evident that these expectations have, at

Table 25. Response Related to Interviewer Expectations of General Difficulty and Level of Respondent Reporting

Item	Easy		Neither		Difficult		Ratio of First to Last Column	R^2
	Correct or Over	Under	Correct or Over	Under	Correct or Over	Under		
Ever Drink Beer	85	83	75	78	80	66	1.29	.11
Income	$13,663	$11,290	$14,649	$12,652	$12,424	$10,767	1.27	.06
Ever Drink Liquor	86	83	82	81	83	73	1.18	.04
Intercourse Past Month	70	67	72	68	66	—	—	.04
Ever Drink Wine	86	83	77	82	84	71	1.21	.02
Gambling Scale	1.15	.90	1.07	.90	1.03	.83	1.39	.02
Intoxication Past Year	27	33	32	34	35	23	1.17	.01
Petting and Kissing Past Month	80	66	82	76	69	78	1.03	.01

Note: See the Ns in the two preceding tables for an indication of sample sizes. Numbers are percentage of respondents reporting this behavior, except for income and gambling scale, where means are present.

most, very small effects. In most practical situations, these effects are trivial and could be ignored.

Nevertheless, these findings suggest two ideas for minimizing interviewer effects. First, interviewers who expect a study to be difficult should not be hired for that study. This study used the best interviewers available to NORC and further screened them with a practice interview. Despite this procedure, general-difficulty expectations had some level effects. Second, interviewers should not be trained to expect underreporting. The behaviors measured in this study are underreported, as seen earlier, but telling interviewers to expect underreporting aggravates the problem.

Small sample sizes keep the data in this chapter from being conclusive. This problem is inherent in research about interviewer expectations—few studies are likely to employ hundreds of interviewers. Replication is the only way to establish precisely the nature and magnitude of interviewer-expectation effects.

Chapter Five

Effects of Respondent Anxiety

In the previous chapters, we measured the effects of the task and of interviewers on response. In this and the next chapter, we focus on the respondents themselves. In this chapter, the analysis is based on the respondents' acute and chronic anxiety—that is, the acute anxiety that respondents feel when asked a threatening question and their usual or chronic anxiety level.

We can distinguish two situations in which respondents' motivations to distort their responses might be aroused. The first situation involves questions about behaviors that are illegal or contranormative or about behaviors that, although not socially deviant, are not usually discussed in public without some tension. The second

Note: Adapted from William Locander, "An Investigation of Interview Method, Threat, and Response Distortion," an unpublished doctoral dissertation, Department of Business Administration, University of Illinois, 1974, and Norman M. Bradburn, Seymour Sudman, Ed Blair, and Carol Stocking, "Question Threat and Response Bias," *Public Opinion Quarterly,* 1978, *46* (2), 221–234.

situation involves providing information on topics that have highly desirable answers. The two situations are closely related, since they both involve social definitions of "desirable" behavior, but they differ in one important respect: In the first situation, the report of committing acts is contranormative; in the second, the report of *not* doing something is contranormative. One might characterize the difference as similar to the one between questions about sins of commission and those about sins of omission. One might speculate that answers to questions about sins of commission will be biased toward underreporting, and that questions about sins of omission will be biased toward overreporting.

The conflict between the role demands of the "good respondent" and the tendency to present oneself positively is resolved in the respondents' answers, but, unfortunately, the investigator does not know in any individual case, without independent validation data, which way the conflict was resolved. One can, however, investigate covariation between the perceived social sensitivity of a topic and the responses to questions on that topic to determine the relative magnitude of response variance produced by tendencies toward anxiety reduction and positive self-presentation.

To understand response effects, two research questions are particularly important: (1) How is response related to individual differences and question threat? (2) Does method of administration affect response in light of respondent differences and question threat?

The first question can be addressed by using Spielberger's (1972) notion that trait and state anxiety are important in stimulus situations that are seen as threatening. Individuals high in trait, or chronic, anxiety are more self-deprecatory, and, fearing failure, they might be expected to manifest higher levels of state anxiety in situations that involve threats to self-esteem. In the interview situation, self-esteem maintenance might result in overreporting socially desirable behaviors or underreporting personal failures. However, threats to self-esteem are individual in nature, so that people vary in the kinds of things they perceive as fear-arousing (Miller and Hewgill, 1966). For example, the person who responds to a threatening mailed questionnaire is different from a person who answers a nonthreatening one (Heybee, 1969; Leibler, 1967).

There is support for Spielberger's hypothesis that trait, or chronic, anxiety is a predisposition to respond to state, or acute, anxiety situations that involve failure or threats to self-esteem (Gorsuch, 1969; Hodges and Felling, 1970). In the threatening-question situation, trait and state anxiety can be used to examine respondents' reactions to the possibility of loss of self-esteem.

The second question can be answered by simply examining the method of administration and threat main effects. In addition, one needs to look at response effects for the chronic and acute groups simultaneously. Since the two variables are very closely related, it is necessary to see if either variable plays a more important role in contributing to response effects as question threat increases.

Design of the Study

The results reported in this chapter are based on the two studies that have been reported and described in Chapters One and Two. For the Chicago sample of eight hundred residents, measures of both chronic and acute anxiety were obtained near the end of the interview. For the national sample of 1,172 adults, the same measures of acute anxiety, but no measures of chronic anxiety, were obtained. As a measure of chronic anxiety, respondents were asked to complete the Bendig Short Form of the Taylor Manifest Anxiety Scale (Bendig, 1956). To measure acute anxiety, two descriptive adjectives, *uneasy* and *annoy*, were used to determine the respondent's postinterview feelings. The measure was developed following the general guidelines of Alexander and Husek (1965), who feel that a measure of acute anxiety must be simple and easily understood by respondents. Gergen and Marlowe (1970) argue that self-report measures in the postexperiment interview are a valid means of determining situational effects.

The wording of the question was: "Questions sometimes have different kinds of effects on people. We'd like your opinions about some of the questions in this interview. As I mention groups of questions, please tell me whether you think those questions would make *most people* very uneasy, moderately uneasy, slightly uneasy, or not at all uneasy. How about the questions on . . . ." There followed a list of topics that were treated in the interview. The indirect form of the question, asking about the respondent's perception of the way *most* people would feel, appears to be a better indicator of uneasiness than direct questions about whether the respondent felt uneasy about the question. The indirect question is in fact a direct question about the respondent's perception of social norms. We interpret the responses as perceptions of the strength of the norms against discussing these topics openly with strangers—in this case, reporting accurately on behavior to an interviewer. As the perceived strength of the norms increases, we would expect there would be greater anxiety about one's self-presentation and thus higher arousal of motives to present oneself favorably and to distort responses in the direction of underreporting.

In addition, we directly asked respondents which of the questions they felt were too personal, and we asked the interviewers to rate the questions for difficulty in the interview. We also have a behavior measure in the proportion of respondents who declined to answer the questions with differing levels of threat.

Results of the National Study

Looking first at the national study, Table 26 presents the ratings for the different question topics. They are ordered by increasing frequency of uneasiness, that is, the perceived strength of the norms against discussing the topics freely. The second and third columns of the table give the interviewer reports of the percentage of respondents for whom the question topic caused difficulty in the interview and the proportion of the respondents who reported (on an open-ended question) that the indicated question topic was too personal. In the final column are the behavioral data—that is, the proportion of the respondents who refused to give any answer to the questions in that topic area. For those areas in which there were multiple questions about activities (for example, social activities), the figure is the average no-answer for the battery of questions. If the questions were filtered ("Did you do X in the past year; if 'yes,' in the last month?"), the no-answer proportion is for the first question in the series.

Our plan in selecting the question topics was to cover a range of normative strength. The ratings by the respondents indicate that we succeeded in selecting questions that practically no one believed would make people very uneasy. Although the interviewer reports

Table 26. Percentage of Ratings of Question Topics

Question Topics	Make Most People Very Uneasy (R's Rating)	Caused Difficulty in Interview (Interviewer Rating)	Question Too Personal (R's Rating)	No Answer on Actual Question
Sports Activities	1	0	0	.1
Leisure Time and General Leisure Activities	2	0	0	.2
Social Activities	2	4	0	.8
Occupation	3	3	2	.1
Education	3	2	1	.3
Happiness and Well-Being	4	6	2	.3
Drinking Beer, Wine, or Liquor	10	10	3	.1
Gambling with Friends	10	3	2	.2
Income	12	9	6	4.8
Petting or Kissing	20	19	0	.3
Getting Drunk	29	9	2	2.3
Using Stimulants or Depressants	31	12	{3}	.1
Using Marijuana or Hashish	42	10	{3}	.4
Sexual Intercourse	42	27	{34}	6.0
Masturbation	56	29	{34}	6.7

Note: N = 1,172, but actual N varies slightly from question to question because of no answers.

of difficulty with questions are generally lower than respondents' ratings of their threat, the rank order of difficulty and uneasiness is very close (rho = .89). The respondents' reports about which questions were too personal *for them* show little variance. Only the sexual-behavior questions were reported to be too personal by a substantial proportion. The behavioral measure of threat—refusal to answer a question—also reveals very little variance among the question topics. Only sexual behavior and income show any substantial number of "no" answers, and these are far below both the uneasiness ratings and the interviewers' reports of difficulty. Such data suggest that the proportion of "no" answers is not a very good indicator of the potential threat of a question.

The income question appears to be a special kind of question, in that it departs furthest in its ranking by the other measures from the general normative ratings given by the respondents. It is about in the middle in respondents' ratings of uneasiness and in the interviewers' ratings of difficulty, but it is the second highest in respondents' perceptions of too-personal questions (although way behind sex) and has the second highest no-answer rate. If "don't knows" are combined with "no" answers, income is the most troublesome of the standard social-characteristic questions typically used in surveys.

There are several ways to react to a question that causes anxiety about answering truthfully. Respondents can refuse to answer the question at all, indicating they feel that the question is inappropriate in the context of the interview, or they can distort answers in the direction of the more socially desirable or less ego-threatening response. For the questions used in this study, we assume the direction of distortion to be denial of engagement in activities when the respondent has in fact done so. To make it easier for respondents to refuse individual questions, we told them at the beginning of the interview that some of the questions we were going to ask might make them feel uneasy and that they need not answer any particular question if they did not want to. In spite of this introduction, as we have seen in Table 26, very few respondents refused to answer even the most threatening questions.

It seems likely that, instead of refusing outright, many respondents simply reported that they did not engage in some particular activity when they in fact did, thereby resolving their dilemma of being good respondents by answering the question but still presenting positive self-pictures to the interviewer. We suspect that such a tendency would be particularly marked among those who feel that there are strong norms against discussing such topics in an interview situation. We can test this hypothesis by looking separately at the distribution of responses to the behavior items for those who rated each of the topics as making most people very uneasy. If the respondents resolved their dilemma in the way that we have suggested, we should find that those who rated the question topic as making most people very uneasy also reported less behavior in that category.

For the most part, the data support this expectation (Table 27). Those who reported that most people would feel very uneasy about answering questions on a particular topic were less likely to report having engaged in that behavior than were people who said that most people would feel only moderately or slightly uneasy about the question. For example, of the 120 respondents who reported that most people would be made very uneasy by questions on gambling, 11 percent reported that they had played cards for money during the past year, as compared with 32 percent of the 419 respondents who reported that most people would be made slightly uneasy by questions about gambling. Combining across all gambling activities, those respondents saying "very uneasy" reported an average of .49 gambling activities in the past year, as compared with an average of 1.13 gambling activities reported by respondents who said questions on gambling would make most people slightly uneasy. Those who felt that most people would be not at all uneasy about answering the question showed an inconsistent pattern, a finding to which we shall return later. For the question about satisfaction with life as a whole, on which we would expect overreporting, we did find that those few who felt such questions would make people feel very uneasy were more likely to report being very satisfied than those in the moderately or slightly category but not than those in the not-at-all category.

This pattern of reporting does not vary much for respondents with different socioeconomic and demographic backgrounds. Sex, race, income, occupation, region, and city size have no effect. Education and age have effects, but the differences in reporting across education and age groups do not form an interpretable pattern.

One important point must be made about the findings. The effect of rating a topic as having high normative threat tends to show up only in the first question about the topic, which is typically: "Have you ever used/done . . . ?" If the respondent replies "yes," then a series of questions about frequency or quantity of behavior follows. Normative threat appears to act as a screen, so that those who report uneasiness about the topic select themselves out of the entire battery of questions by simply saying that they have never done or used the subject of the questions. If, however, they admit having used or done the thing asked about, level of uneasiness does not appear to influence reports of frequency or quantity of behavior. In Chapter Two, we saw that question structure (open or closed) and length (of introduction) have an important effect on reports of frequency and amount of behavior, given that the respondent admits having engaged in the behavior at all. The question-wording variables, however, were not related to the initial reports of ever having engaged in the behavior.

Thus, it appears that a two-step process affects reports of behaviors perceived as threatening. In the first step, respondents who may have engaged in the behaviors but find it contranormative to discuss this in the interview situation resolve the role conflict between being a good respondent and presenting a positive self-image by denying that they have ever engaged in the behavior. In the second step, the question wording encourages or discourages efforts to report accurately the extent of the behavior.

The differences in reporting are mainly between those who report that most people would be very uneasy in talking about a particular topic and all others. In some cases, however, particularly among those questions that deal with topics rated as more threatening, those reporting that most people would be not at all uneasy in discussing the topic should also have lower levels of reporting actual behavior. To this finding we now turn.

The Nonthreatened Respondent

In hypothesizing a relationship between normative threat and behavioral underreporting, we assumed that there was no relationship between perceived normative threat and a person's behavior—that is, we assumed that respondents' perceptions of the

Table 27. Reported Behavior by Level of Uneasiness About Question

Topics	Percentage of Those Who Felt . . . Who Reported			
	Very Uneasy	Moderately Uneasy	Slightly Uneasy	Not at All Uneasy
Average Number of Sports Activities	.60 (15)	1.00 (26)	1.36 (74)	2.09 (1042)
Average Number of Leisure Activities	4.42 (28)	5.04 (79)	5.36 (121)	5.80 (932)
Happiness and Well-Being (Very Satisfied with Life)	29.00 (41)	18.00 (117)	21.00 (432)	33.00 (558)
Gambling				
Played Cards for Money	11.00 (120)	30.00 (155)	32.00 (419)	34.00 (456)
Bet on Sports	8.00	16.00	21.00	20.00
Bet on Elections	3.00	12.00	10.00	11.00
Betting Pool	5.00	18.00	19.00	18.00
Played Dice	3.00	6.00	7.00	8.00
Bought Lottery Ticket	18.00	20.00	24.00	27.00
Average Number of Gambling Activities	.49	1.01	1.13	1.18
Drinking				
Ever Drink Beer or Ale	67.00 (119)	82.00 (166)	82.00 (432)	80.00 (438)
Ever Drink Wine or Champagne	60.00	82.00	89.00	80.00
Ever Drink Hard Liquor	63.00	84.00	85.00	84.00

Intoxication				
Intoxication Past Year	24.00 (327)	36.00 (233)	38.00 (332)	27.00 (230)
Marijuana				
Ever Smoked Marijuana	18.00 (480)	33.00 (217)	26.00 (220)	15.00 (250)
Drugs				
Ever Use Stimulants	14.00 (359)	15.00 (279)	10.00 (276)	5.00 (231)
Ever Use Depressants	8.00 (359)	14.00 (279)	29.00 (276)	6.00 (231)
Sex				
Petting and Kissing Past Month	63.00 (224)	81.00 (281)	78.00 (340)	71.00 (301)
Petting and Kissing, No Answer	7.00	3.00	2.00	1.00
Intercourse Past Month	59.00 (474)	75.00 (296)	75.00 (209)	53.00 (167)
Intercourse Past Month, No Answer	9.00	4.00	1.00	2.00
Masturbation Past Month	10.00 (630)	11.00 (208)	7.00 (148)	8.00 (132)
Masturbation Past Month, No Answer	6.00	4.00	4.00	2.00

Note: Statistical tests of significance are not reported on these data, because we are not testing hypotheses in the strict sense and are using hypotheses suggested by the data. See Kruskal (1968, pp. 247–255).

norms about talking about certain kinds of behavior were independent of whether they had actually engaged in such behavior. This
assumption includes the notion that the norms are "social facts" that
are more or less accurately and uniformly known. We expected that
the probability of a particular type of behavior actually occurring
would be equal across all categories of response about the normative threat of that type of behavior. Thus, when we observe that
the proportion of people who report engaging in some particular
behavior is lower in one response category, we interpret this
as evidence of underreporting rather than as evidence of a real
difference.

 This assumption of the independence of the perception of
social norms and actual behavior is, however, somewhat tenuous
when applied to behavior that is more seriously contranormative.
People who have not engaged in the behavior may have a "clear
conscience" and estimate other people's willingness to talk about the
topic differently from those who have engaged in the behavior and
have a "guilty conscience." In this case, there would be an interaction
between the perceived normative threat and the respondents' own
behavior, such that their own behavior becomes part of the determinant of the perceived norms.

 If there were such an interaction between the respondents'
actual behavior and their perception of norms about discussing the
topic with strangers, we would expect that the occurrence of a
contranormative behavior would really be higher for respondents
with higher perceptions of general uneasiness. That is, among respondents who report that most people would be not at all uneasy
about discussing a topic, a smaller proportion would actually engage
in the behavior than would be the case among respondents who
report that most people would feel slightly uneasy, moderately uneasy, or very uneasy. Underreporting by respondents who report
"very uneasy" would cause a nonmonotonic relationship between
reported behavior and perceived uneasiness, with reported behavior rising and then falling across uneasiness categories.

 Such a nonmonotonic relationship is what we find for topics
that 20 percent or more of the respondents rated as making most
people very uneasy. In response to these topics, we find the proportions of respondents reporting the behavior to be lower for both of

the two extreme groups—"very uneasy" and "not-at-all uneasy"—than for the intermediate categories. If our interaction hypothesis is true, the lower behavioral reports among those who say "very uneasy" are primarily due to underreporting, and the lower reports among the "not-at-all uneasy" are primarily due to real differences in behavior. Although such an interpretation is plausible, we do not have any external validation data to test this hypothesis.

Revised Estimates of Threatening Events

Assuming that respondents who report that a question would make most people very uneasy are underreporting their behavior in that area provides a simple method for improving estimates of threatening behaviors. Revised estimates may be obtained either by assuming that very uneasy respondents behave like all other respondents or by assuming that very uneasy respondents behave like moderately uneasy respondents.

For the gambling, drinking, and petting and kissing questions, the revised estimates are 2 to 8 percent higher than the initial estimates. For the more threatening intoxication, marijuana, and sexual-intercourse questions, the revised estimates exceed the original estimates by larger amounts, from 8 percent for the sexual-intercourse question to 27 percent for the marijuana questions. These larger differences occur because a larger fraction of the sample reports being very uneasy about these questions, so that the impact on the overall estimate is greater.

Common sense suggests that revised estimates incorporating supplementary information about uneasiness are improved estimates. Obviously, one would like direct proof that revision is improvement, but in this study we could not get validating evidence. The study described in the next section did have such validation information available from record checks. Respondents who reported that questions about traffic violations and declaration of bankruptcy would make most people very uneasy reported only 27 percent of validated events as compared with about 75 percent for respondents who perceived these questions as less threatening. Even respondents who reported that these extremely threatening questions would make most people somewhat uneasy or not at all uneasy underreported behavior. Use of a supplementary question on perceived threat provides an improved estimate but not an unbiased estimate.

It may be interesting to compare this estimation technique with randomized response procedures used for estimating threatening behavior. Randomized response procedures assume that respondents will tell the truth if their anonymity is guaranteed by use of the randomized response mechanism. Some evidence shows that randomized response procedures do improve estimates, but other evidence shows that response effects do remain. In Chapter One, for example, we saw that 35 percent of those respondents who had been arrested for drunken driving did not report this arrest when using a randomized response procedure. Randomized response methods and the use of supplementary information on perceived threat both yield improved but not perfect estimates, and both methods make assumptions about respondent behavior that are partially but not completely true (see also Reinmuth and Geurts, 1975).

Comparison with Other Data

Table 28 compares both the unadjusted and adjusted estimates from the previous section to some comparative data from other sources. Since the different experimental forms did have effects on the number of times behaviors were reported once the respondent had admitted them (see Chapter Two), the estimates for some of the items are given separately by form.

In general, the unadjusted data are very similar to results from other surveys. As examples, a national study conducted by Temple University's Institute of Social Research (Wilson, 1975) estimated that 68.8 percent of adults had engaged in intercourse in the past month, and the unadjusted estimate from this study is 68.6 percent. It was estimated that 19 percent of respondents had ever smoked marijuana in a national study conducted by the Response Analysis Corporation (Abelson and Atkinson, 1975), as compared with 21.7 percent in this study.

Adjusted estimates are larger than comparative surveys, indicating that current estimates are somewhat low. That current estimates are low can be seen in the estimates for beer, wine, and liquor consumed, where even the adjusted estimates using the best forms understate sales by at least one fourth. Our study did not ask how

Item	Unadjusted	Adjusted[a]	Comparison Data
Engaged in Intercourse Past Month	68.6%	74.0%	68.8%[b]
Mean Annual Frequency of Intercourse (All Adults)			
Long, Open Forms	90	101	
Short, Closed Forms	72	79	76[b]
Ever Smoked Marijuana	21.7%	27.6%	19%[c]
Number of Times Drank Beer Past Year (for Adults Who Drank Beer Past Month)			
Long, Open Form	124	126	
Short, Closed Form	73	74	82.41[d]
Number of Times Drank Wine Past Year (for Adults Who Drank Wine Past Month)			
Long, Open Form	77	76	
Short, Closed Form	47	49	42.95[d]
Number of Times Drank Liquor Past Year (for Adults Who Drank Liquor Past Month)			
Long, Open Form	68	65	
Short, Closed Form	48	49	56.21[d]
Ounces of Beer Consumed Per Capita Past Year (All Adults)			
Long, Open Form	2,046	2,099	
Short, Closed Form	1,163	1,173	3,982[e]
Ounces of Wine Consumed Per Capita Past Year (All Adults)			
Long, Open Form	206	225	
Short, Closed Form	104	106	304[e]
Ounces of Liquor Consumed Per Capita Past Year (All Adults)			
Long, Open Form	86	87	
Short, Closed Form	65	67	234[e]

[a]The "very uneasy" group has been given the mean of the "moderately uneasy" group as an adjustment.
[b]Wilson (1975).
[c]Abelson and Atkinson (1975).
[d]Harris and Associates, Inc. (1974).
[e]U.S. Brewers Association (1975).

many ounces of beer, wine, and liquor were consumed, but how many glasses. As noted in Chapter Two, the conversion to ounces was made by assuming that the average wine glass contained three ounces. Similarly, it was assumed that a glass or can of beer contained twelve ounces, and that a drink of liquor contained one ounce.

Results of the Chicago Study

Although the Chicago study was done earlier than the national study, it is presented later, since it deals not only with acute anxiety, but with the relation between acute and chronic anxiety. The reader should recall that in this study, discussed in Chapter One, validation data are available for the measured questions.

Drawing from the literature on anxiety and response effects, we formulated three hypotheses:

- H_1: Respondents with high acute-anxiety scores distort responses significantly more than those with low scores.
- H_2: The method of question administration is significantly more important when the respondent perceives question threat as high.
- H_3: Respondents with high chronic-anxiety scores distort responses significantly more than those with low scores.

The first hypothesis is based on the question-threat literature, which suggests that respondents with high acute scores perceive the questions as highly threatening and therefore distort responses. The focus of the first hypothesis is on the respondent's perception of the question itself. The second hypothesis was derived from the interviewing literature, in which the interview situation is seen as being composed of task and social involvement (see Sudman and Bradburn, 1974). Task involvement refers to answering the questions posed by the interviewer. The social element is seen as involvement with the interviewer as a personality. When a personal question is posed, the respondent reacts not only to the question but to the interviewer's presence. From these theoretical considerations, researchers have argued that method of administration is an important influence when gathering personal data. To examine these notions more closely, the measures of anxiety were analyzed with respect to methods of administration. The third hypothesis is based on the Spielberger (1972) notion that respondents with high chronic anxiety tend to perceive things as more threatening than an objective evaluation would rate their potential threat. Such perceptions, in turn, cause higher proportions of distortion for the high-chronic group. Hypothesis three also addresses the relationship between individual-difference effects and distortion.

Before testing the hypotheses, it was necessary to examine the relationship between the acute- and chronic-anxiety scores. The correlations between the chronic measure and four acute measures ranged from $-.178$ to $-.065$. These slightly negative correlations support Spielberger's argument that trait and state anxiety are related by separate constructs.

For each topic in this study—having a library card, voting, drunken driving, and bankruptcy—respondents were asked not only how uneasy they thought the questions would make most people feel but also how much they thought the questions would annoy most people. Acute-anxiety scores were derived by summing (very = 3, somewhat = 2, and not at all = 1) the responses for the "uneasy" and "annoy" questions. Acute groups were formed by classifying respondents with additive scores of 5 or 6 in the high group, those with 3 or 4 in the medium-acute group, and those with 1 or 2 in the low group. This was done for all questions except the one about having a library card, where the "uneasy" scale was used directly.

The data in Table 29 show the percentage of individuals responding to the acute-anxiety scales by question type. The library-card and voting-behavior questions produced quite small percentages in the "very" category, and the court and traffic questions had a number of respondents who were very or somewhat uneasy or annoyed by these parts of the survey. Another interesting finding in Table 29 pertains to the random response model, which is supposed to reduce the anxiety of particular threatening questions in the survey. As can be seen from the table, for the most part the model produced percentages greater than or equal to the other methods, especially for the higher-threat questions.

Table 30 shows the proportion of distorted responses by method and acute group. In this study, distortion is defined as the

Theodore Lownik Library
Illinois Benedictine College
Lisle, Illinois 60532

Table 29. Percentage of Individuals Responding to the "Uneasy" and "Annoy" Acute-Anxiety Questions

Method	Scale	Library Card	Voting		Court		Traffic	
		Uneasy	Uneasy	Annoy	Uneasy	Annoy	Uneasy	Annoy
Personal Interview	Very	2.2	2.2	3.2	15.7	18.9	15.1	12.1
	Somewhat	12.9	17.2	19.5	60.5	59.4	39.3	51.5
	Not at All	84.9	79.5	78.2	23.6	21.6	45.4	36.3
Telephone	Very	0	1.1	4.2	14.6	14.6	8.6	6.5
	Somewhat	9.2	26.0	23.4	63.4	56.0	52.1	41.3
	Not at All	90.7	72.9	72.3	21.9	29.2	39.1	52.1
Self-Administered	Very	1.2	0	2.3	9.0	11.7	3.8	0
	Somewhat	8.2	18.6	19.0	45.4	41.1	34.6	44.4
	Not at All	90.6	81.3	78.6	48.5	47.0	61.5	55.6
Random Response	Very	1.1	5.8	6.9	18.9	13.9	12.1	9.1
	Somewhat	6.6	16.2	16.3	59.4	52.8	51.5	51.5
	Not at All	92.2	77.9	76.7	21.6	33.3	36.3	39.4
N (Average Cell Size per Column)		91	90	89	37	37	35	35

Table 30. Proportion of Distortion by Method of Administration and Acute Groups

| | Acute Anxiety | | | |
Method	High	Medium	Low	Mean
Personal Interview	.50	.24	.28	.34
	(28)	(63)	(141)	
Telephone	.41	.34	.21	.32
	(34)	(88)	(124)	
Self-Administered	.47	.30	.24	.34
	(34)	(43)	(132)	
Mean	.46	.29	.25	

difference between the response and the validation divided by the total sample size. The random response model was deleted from this part of the study, because it is designed to estimate population parameters by picking one of two questions using a probability mechanism. In essence, the interviewer does not even know which question is being answered. Therefore, any one respondent's answer could not be validated. (The random response model is discussed in Chapter One.)

The results in Table 30 show little difference in the overall proportion of distortion across interview methods. However, dramatic effects can be seen for the high-acute group, which had a 46 percent distortion rate, as compared with 29 percent and 25 percent for the medium-acute and low-acute groups. This difference was tested using Tukey's analysis of variance test for $N = 1$ (Kirk, 1968). The analysis of variance was calculated for both raw proportions and arcsine-transformed data. The results did not vary from one to the other. The ANOVA findings showed that the method effect ($F = .072$) was not significant, but the acute-anxiety effect was significant at the 0.05 level ($F = 7.78$). Thus, hypothesis one was accepted.

The second hypothesis can be rejected on the basis of the findings reported in Table 30. The insignificant method effect reported above reveals that, although the high-acute group distorted significantly more than the other two acute groups, the presence or absence of an interviewer made little difference in terms of response distortion. This finding is another confirmation of the finding, noted in Chapter One, that respondents, regardless of anxiety level, are not sensitive to the "personalness" of the method by which the survey is administered.

The third hypothesis stated that respondents high in chronic anxiety have higher distortion rates than the low-chronic group. Based on the results of the Bendig Short Form of the Taylor Manifest Anxiety Scale (Bendig, 1956), subjects were divided into high-, medium-, and low-chronic groups. The respective score ranges were from 9–19 (high), 3–8 (medium), and 0–2 (low). These groups were chosen at natural breaks in the distribution. The range for each group was not substantially different from those reported by Sarason (1959).

An analysis of variance for $N = 1$ showed that the chronic-anxiety effect was *not* significant for any of the three methods of administration. However, when the chronic variable was examined across the threat dimension, an interesting finding became apparent. Table 31 shows the cell and average proportions of distortion of both low- and high-threat questions. For the lower-threat library-card and voting-behavior items, the high-chronic-anxiety group distorts about 10 percent more than the low and medium group. The high-threat questions, bankruptcy and drunken driving, show little difference between low and high chronics, with the mediums recording the highest proportion of distortion (.45).

Chronic anxiety appears to operate for only the lower-threat questions, where acute anxiety has a minimum effect. When high-threat questions are presented, the chronic and acute effects produce an inverted-U effect. That is, the medium-chronics are the respondents who react most defensively by distorting their responses.

Another important consideration in analyzing the results in Table 31 is the nature of the report that respondents are required to make. That is, did the question require an overreport or underreport answer? Overreporting refers to questions in which the respondent answers in the socially desirable direction (voter registration, library card, and primary voter) when in fact the respondent has not so behaved. Underreporting refers to denying an undesirable act (bankruptcy and drunken driving) when the respondent did

Table 31. Proportions of Distortion for Chronic-Anxiety Group by Low's High-Threat Questions

Chronic Anxiety	Low Threat			
	Register to Vote	Vote in Primary	Library Card	Average
Low	.09	.36	.13	.19
				(41)
Medium	.16	.29	.21	.22
				(145)
High	.19	.48	.20	.29
				(47)

Chronic Anxiety	High Threat		
	Bankruptcy	Drunk Driving	Average
Low	.28	.37	.32
			(21)
Medium	.37	.53	.45
			(40)
High	.27	.36	.31
			(27)

commit the behavior. The relationship between question-threat level and the nature of the report needs further examination in future research efforts. However, the data did suggest that the two distinct types of questions should be considered when dealing with the problem of minimizing response effects.

Conclusions

It is evident from the results of both studies that the perceived normative threat of a topic influences responses to questions. Respondents who report that questions about an activity would make most people very uneasy are less likely to report ever engaging in that activity than are persons who respond with only "moderately uneasy." Perceived threat thus acts as a gatekeeper to prevent further questions.

If respondents admit that they participate in an activity, perceived threat appears to have no effect on the level of activity reported. Although the effects of perceived threat on response are important, they are smaller than the effects of question structure, which do change levels of reported activity.

Since perceived threat causes underreporting, some simple adjustment methods may be used to improve estimates of threatening behavior. These assume that respondents who report being very uneasy are at least as likely to participate in an activity as those who report being moderately uneasy or all other respondents.

Chapter Six

Reinterpreting the Marlowe-Crowne Scale

In previous chapters, we have presented various ways of measuring response bias and recommendations about how to reduce such bias or how to adjust data to minimize the effects of such bias in analysis. The material in those chapters focused on ways to improve questionnaire design or method of administration to reduce response bias for all respondents in a survey. In this chapter, we will examine a scale—the Marlowe-Crowne Social Desirability Scale (Crowne and Marlowe, 1960, 1964)—that has been used in survey research to identify particular respondents who are most

Note: Adapted from Carol Stocking, "Marlowe-Crowne Scale in Survey Research: A Sociological Interpretation," unpublished doctoral dissertation, Department of Sociology, University of Chicago, 1978.

likely to distort their answers to survey questions in a socially desirable direction. The Marlowe-Crowne scale (or subsections of it) has been used in surveys administered to nearly 10,000 respondents in half a dozen major research projects. In most of these studies, the scale has been used only as a measure of the tendency to answer survey questions in a falsely positive manner. Few people would argue that no one falsely disclaims illegal or contranormative behavior in an interview situation, or that there are no persons who paint falsely glowing pictures of their lives during a survey interview. The question addressed in this chapter is whether we can discover such people in survey samples by administering the Marlowe-Crowne scale as a measure of the tendency to distort during the interview itself.

Design of the Study

The research reported in this chapter is based on the nationwide study described in Chapter Two. In addition to questions about leisure-time activities, which were designed to progress from the innocuous (for example, going window shopping) to the contranormative (for example, using marijuana), respondents were asked a subset of ten Marlowe-Crowne scale items. The Marlowe-Crowne Social Desirability Scale (also called the need-for-approval or MC scale) was originally designed to measure the need within respondents to gain the approval of the experimenter in psychological test situations. David Crowne and Douglas Marlowe (1960) developed the original thirty-three-item scale in the context of their attempt to understand the poor predictive power of personality tests.

The scale consists of statements that are either socially desirable but untrue of virtually everyone (for example, "I never resent being asked to return a favor") or socially undesirable but true of almost everyone (for example, "At times, I have really insisted on having things my own way"). MC scores are simply the total number of answers in the scaled direction. Marlowe and Crowne and others subsequently carried out a large number of social-psychological experiments exploring the implications of high scores on the MC scale in various areas of behavior.

Other researchers (for example, Clancy, 1971; Gove and Geerken, 1977; Campbell, Converse, and Rodgers, 1976; and

Smith, 1967), have used the MC scale to identify respondents who may be distorting survey responses. The questions examined ranged from a fairly direct parallel of some of the social-psychological research (for example, using the MC scale in community mental health surveys with questions that resemble those on personality inventories), to extending those concepts to any statements that might be considered to give favorable or unfavorable impressions of the respondent to the interviewer (such as reports about feelings of happiness or unhappiness), and finally to defining any items in a survey that correlate with high MC scores as probable targets for misreporting (for example, reports of regular doctor visits are thus defined as image-enhancing).

Marlowe and Crowne and their colleagues continued to work with the scale and developed an interpretation that included differences in real-world behavior between those with high and low scores (see especially Conn and Crowne, 1964; Fishman, 1965; Strahan and Strahan, 1972; and Strickland and Lewicki, 1966). The bulk of this research suggests that, although there may be intrapsychic adjustments associated with MC scores, these are profound and persistent and are reflected in a wide range of real-world behaviors and attitudes.

Our research pursues the more developed Marlowe-Crowne interpretation. The question we address is whether persons who score high on the Marlowe-Crowne scale should be assumed to be the persons who are most likely to distort responses to other questions in a socially desirable direction, or whether in fact they tend to behave in a more socially desirable fashion.

The Marlowe-Crowne scale has not been given much attention as a dependent variable in survey data, and no theory has been advanced about why some people would seek to create a favorable impression during the interview and others would not. Throughout this chapter, we use the phrase "during the interview" as a shorthand term that might include all interactions with relative strangers. Campbell, Converse, and Rodgers (1976) suggest that we think of this bias as the difference between responses given to the interviewer and those that would be given to close friends, if they asked the same questions. The critical distinction is whether the respondent says one thing to the interviewer but has a different privately held attitude or falsely reports behavior. The sociological literature does not report attempts to define what the MC scale may measure—whether it measures behavior limited to the interview situation, whether it extends to all behavior with strangers, or whether the behavior associated with the scale may be more extensive than that.

The MC scale consists of a series of categorical statements. Reports of always or never behaving in some fashion are the basis of high MC scores. Would a special style of thinking be generated for responding to the MC scale, or might that style of thinking be continuous and pervasive? If such thinking is pervasive, we would expect it to be reflected in attitudes. Further, persons with high scores may tend to see the world in terms of absolutes and be more likely to have rigid standards for their own behavior (and that of others). It is likely that such persons behave differently from persons with more relativistic standards. It is possible that the differences in behavior and attitudes reported by respondents with high MC scores reflect real differences in the ways people think about norms, judge their own behavior, and act in the real world.

To evaluate whether the differences between persons with high and low MC scores are part of the real variance in our data or are a component of the error variance, we examined the data with this question in mind. Our general strategy was to determine whether there were differences that could not be reasonably explained in terms of image management. We examined general activities, sociability, drinking, intoxication, and marijuana use to evaluate whether the differences in reported behavior associated with MC scores should be assumed to be part of the true variance or the error variance.

MC Scores and Background Variables

Looking at the MC scale as a dependent variable, we find that it is a relatively poor measure—the average interitem correlation is only .09 (with reliability estimated at .497). The literature suggested that this would be the case; the reliability of .88 reported by Marlowe and Crowne was based on a thirty-three-item scale. The actual items in the subset we used were selected by Clancy (1971). Although he did it on the basis of an item analysis, an actual reading of the items suggests that they are somewhat unsuited to a national sample. For example, sneaking into a movie seems particularly age-linked. The item "No matter who I'm talking to, I'm always a good listener" is somewhat contradictory. Although the scale has weaknesses, it provides some interesting findings, if not always the findings that other response-bias researchers would have anticipated.

The MC scale is strongly related to age and to education, so that older, less-educated people tend to have higher MC scores, as do persons who live outside of metropolitan areas and persons with lower incomes (see Table 32). The interpretation of this information might be that persons with less education or lower incomes simply act on the norms of deference in our society when they falsely claim positive attitudes to the interviewer, who is perceived to be of higher status. Similarly, persons in small towns may see the interviewer as a sophisticated person worthy of deference. Deference in this case would mean telling interviewers what they want to hear—that you always behave in socially desirable ways and that you are happy, satisfied, and enjoying the interview.

However, the strongest correlation, with age, is more difficult to explain in this context. Why would older people tend to distort their answers to survey questions? Why would older people describe themselves so positively in terms of the scale items? We interpret this as primarily a cohort effect—that is, older people tend to think in categorical terms about rules for behavior, because they are more likely to have been brought up to think in such terms. (There may also be an aging effect, but the cohort effect gives the baseline from which one may move to more categorical thinking. In our view, that baseline has become more relativistic since the early decades of the century, and the aging effect is unlikely to move subsequent cohorts as far as the older people in our sample toward the categorical

Table 32. Correlations of the MC Scale with Independent Variables

Age	.337	(.481)[a]
Education	−.261	(−.372)
Family Income	−.181	(−.258)
Size of Town	−.103	(−.147)
Race	.065	
Sex	.022	
Marital Status	.261	(Eta)

[a]Correlations in parentheses corrected for attenuation.

extreme.) By agreeing with the categorical statements that compose the MC scale, older people are in fact demonstrating the way they actually think about their own behavior and attitudes. They are not claiming virtues for the benefit of the interviewer; they think of themselves as always helpful, never resentful, and so on. Further, not only older persons, but also those who live outside of metropolitan areas and those who have less education or lower incomes are more likely to adhere to older norms. An uncritical acceptance of these norms pervades their attitudes and behavior in the real world (as well as in the interview situation).

No theoretical reason has been advanced to account for the relationship between MC scores and marital status originally reported in several studies (Campbell, Converse, and Rodgers, 1976; Clancy and Gove, 1974; and Gove and Geerken, 1977) by persons who interpret the MC scale to be a measure of response bias. After looking at Table 33, one might suggest that widows and widowers, isolated after companionship, are especially dependent on the approval of the interviewer and thus distort their responses to the MC items. One would then also have to assume that the never-married respondents, accustomed to their isolation, do not try to curry favor with the interviewer. One could make quite a plausible interpretation along these lines, but the resulting interpretation presents serious problems for the overall theory. If the widowed are so anxious to gain favor from the interviewer, how could one assume that such attempts would be limited to the interview situation? Would not the need to gain approval extend into their everyday lives and affect the way they interact with people in general? Similarly, would the

Table 33. MC Scores by Marital Status

	Score[a]	Adjusted for Age[a]	Adjusted for Age and Education[a]
Never Married	−.96	−.57	−.50
Divorced and Separated	−.13	−.15	−.15
Currently Married	+.12	+.10	+.10
Widowed	+1.10	+.48	+.37
	(Eta = .26)	(Beta = .14)	(Beta = .12)

[a]Expressed as deviations from the mean. Grand Mean = 5.90.

never-married not be free to act without considering the reactions of others? Once admitting that the motivation to gain approval from the interviewer (or the freedom not to gain approval) extends outside the interview situation, the case for considering the MC scale as a measure of bias is considerably weakened. The critical underlying assumption of this interpretation of the variable is that MC scores do not in fact correlate with real behavior or true attitudes at all.

We have, however, assumed that MC scores reflect a persistent way of thinking about norms that would be widely evidenced in real-world attitudes and behavior. We consider that persons who think of themselves as helpful to those in trouble, willing to return favors, not insistent about having their own way, and so on, are likely to behave differently from people who have no such need. Further, we suggest that such differences in goals for behavior and actual behavior may be functional for maintaining marriages. Let us start by proposing that some intrapsychic adjustments represented by MC scores are functional for initiating and maintaining marriages. We could then assume that the never-married would tend to have the lowest MC scores. Persons who have married and then separated or divorced would have the next lowest scores. Since this category would include some persons who have the psychological characteristics associated with initiating or causing separation, and others who have the characteristics for potentially maintaining marriages, we expect that this group mean is somewhat raised by the latter subgroup. The currently married group would also include some persons who will initiate separations, and that subgroup would slightly lower the mean MC scores of the group, which would still be about average. Finally, we could view the widowed as having had successful marriages, since they lasted until the death of one partner, and would expect that group to have the highest MC scores. In this way, we would account for the ordering of mean MC scores associated with those marital statuses (Table 33).

We still do not know whether the psychological concomitants of MC scores are functional for initiating marriage or whether those psychological factors develop during marriage and help to maintain it. We do not know whether divorced persons entered their marriages with lower than average MC scores or whether they failed to make the intrapsychic adjustments indicated by higher MC scores that assist in maintaining marriage. It may be that persons who have never married have had less need to see themselves as living up to certain rules. However, if we look at age as a rough surrogate for length of marriage, we see that the mean of the currently married group is reduced very little when the effects of age are removed (Table 33). If we look at mean MC scores of the married and never-married in terms of age groups (Table 34), we see that the ratios are constant, and we cannot assume that maintaining marriages raises the MC scores in Column A. However, either the aging process or a cohort effect is visible in both sets of means. Whether married or not, older people have higher scores.

Our interpretation of this finding is that the real-world behavior of people with higher MC scores is sufficiently different from that of persons with lower scores so that the traits that are measured affect the likelihood of getting married and staying married. It stands to reason that such behavior would be cooperative—possibly altruistic—rather than egoistic.

Although the response-bias interpretation of the MC variables can account for some of the correlations we have discussed, we can see no plausible reason why older people or married people would have more need for approval from the interviewer than younger or unmarried people. The response-bias interpretation simply cannot account for these strong relationships in our data.

MC Scores, General Activities, and Sociability

To explore the relationship of MC scores and general activities, we constructed a scale by summing responses to seven questions. (The items included were dining in a restaurant, going to a

Table 34. Mean MC Scores of the Married and Never-Married Within Age Groups

	A	B	
	Currently Married	Never Married	$\frac{B}{A}$
35 and Younger	5.472	4.817	.8803
36 to 51	5.914	5.228	.8840
52 and Over	6.726	5.883	.8747

movie, going window shopping, having been on a picnic, taking a ride for pleasure, going for a walk or hike, and going swimming.) The average interitem correlation of the scale is .159, and reliability is estimated as .570. If one imagines that persons with high MC scores distort survey answers to impress the interviewer, one could easily imagine that such persons would overreport participation in wholesome activities. However, there was a negative relationship between the general-activity scale and MC scores, which persisted when age was controlled (Table 35). On the basis of this negative correlation, response-bias researchers would have to conclude that there was something undesirable about reporting these activities to the interviewer. However, the negative correlation fits our theory that persons with high MC scores lead more circumscribed lives. Maintaining older norms requires insulation from new and different experiences and from people who behave differently. We do not think that failure to participate in these activities causes high MC scores; rather, we think that high scores are more easily maintained with a somewhat restricted scope of life. Although the effect is modest, activity is related to MC scores in the way that we predicted.

Those who view MC scores as indications of response bias must agree that persons with high scores do not inflate reports of acceptable activities to enhance their image with the interviewer, nor can they claim that bland inattention leads persons with high scores to respond "yes" to simple questions to appear agreeable. Finally, we can see no grounds for suggesting that, since persons with high scores do not report these activities, the activities must somehow appear to them to be unacceptable to admit to the interviewer. The response-bias theory cannot account for the negative relationships between MC scores and general activities found in our data.

Table 35. MC Scores for Various Activity Levels

	Number	Score[a]	Score Adjusted for Age[a]
0 to 2 Activities	277	.60	.25
3 to 4 Activities	440	.12	.09
5 to 7 Activities	447	−.49	−.25
		Eta = .22	Beta = .10

[a]Expressed as deviations from the mean. Grand Mean = 5.90.

To investigate the relationship between social activities and MC scores, we used a somewhat different strategy than we did for general activities (although a scale of social activities constructed in that way is correlated with MC scores at −.19). It is more interesting to look at those social activities that might tend to introduce variety into the social life of the respondent—parties for five or more persons and social evenings outside the neighborhood. We summed the frequency codes for those two questions. The codes range from 2 (about once a year) to 7 (almost every day). Thus, although higher numbers indicate greater frequency, the intervals are not equal. We then divided the sample values approximately into thirds to look at the relationship of this sociability variable to MC scores (Table 36). We see that fewer social contacts are associated with higher MC scores; a small difference persists when we adjust for age.

Those who see the MC scale as an indicator of response bias would probably have to accept the reports about acceptable activities given by persons with high MC scores as true reports of being slightly less active or less sociable than the mean. They might then elaborate on their theory by suggesting that persons with high MC scores would falsely deny unacceptable activities but would not falsely claim acceptable ones to enhance their image with the interviewer. They would still have to deal with the evidence that persons with high scores not only do not seem to overreport acceptable activities, but actually report fewer such activities than do persons with lower scores. Here is further evidence that real-world behavior is related to MC scores. We have accepted this probability from the beginning.

Table 36. MC Scores by Level of Sociability

	Number	Score[a]	Score Adjusted for Age[a]
Less Frequent (0–4)	367	.52	.29
Average (5–6)	361	−.09	−.04
More Frequent (7–13)	436	−.35 Eta = .18	−.21 Beta = .10

[a] Expressed as deviations from the mean. Grand Mean = 5.90.

MC Scores and Drinking Behavior

We assume that persons with high MC scores are less likely to drink alcoholic beverages than persons with lower scores. (The response-bias interpretation is that persons with high scores are as likely to drink as persons with low scores; any differences in reporting drinking behavior would be indications of response bias.)

The general norm about drinking is not clear to us. Although Gallup (1977) reports that 29 percent of a national sample claim to be total abstainers, only 9 percent of our sample report never having used (even once) any form of alcoholic beverage. It is difficult to believe that the general population holds that not drinking is desirable; it seems, rather, that a small minority of persons consider abstinence to be appropriate behavior. Those who hold the response-bias interpretation would assume that persons who falsely deny drinking conceive of abstinence as image-enhancing. It seems to us that the minority who consider abstention to be desirable behavior are in fact the most likely persons to abstain from alcohol.

We constructed a scale that summed reports of drinking behavior. Respondents were given one point if they had been to a tavern or bar in the past year or if they reported having drunk any beer, wine, or liquor during the past year. Scores thus range from 0 (reporting none of these behaviors) to 4 (reporting a visit to a bar and having drunk beer and wine and liquor during the year). We assume that persons who score higher on this scale will have lower mean MC scores. The response-bias interpretation of the MC variable would expect the same results for different reasons. MC scores for each of the levels of the scale are presented in Table 37, and there are differences in MC scores in the predicted direction. It seems reasonable to assume that drinking behavior is related to age, since older persons may have been socialized when liquor was illegal or may have physical problems that inhibit drinking. However, we see that the effects persist when scores are adjusted for age.

Persons who claim not to have drunk alcoholic beverages or to have been in a bar in the past year have MC scores considerably above the mean. If we looked only at Table 37, we might feel justified in asserting that persons with high scores underreport drinking, but we have seen that persons with high MC scores partici-

Table 37. MC Scores by Kinds of Drinking in the Past Year

		Number	Score[a]	Score Adjusted for Age[a]
Did not Drink Beer or Wine	0	203	.97	.70
or Liquor or Go to a Bar	1	122	.28	.13
	2	152	.28	.14
	3	284	−.12	−.07
Drank Beer and Wine and	4	403	−.59	−.40
Liquor and Went to a Bar			Eta = .28	Beta = .19

[a]Expressed as deviations from the mean. Grand Mean = 5.90.

pate less in general activities and social activities. If those differences are real, we would also expect to find real differences in drinking behavior.

MC Scores, Intoxication, and Marijuana Use

The general social norm about drinking behavior is not clear. If there is a general social norm against using alcoholic beverages, it is a norm that 90 percent of the sample claim to have violated at some time in their lives; over 80 percent claim to have used some alcoholic beverage during the year prior to the survey. Asserting that persons would underreport having drunk alcohol during the past year to enhance their image or to maintain their self-esteem in the interview situation seems to attribute false strength to a vanishing norm. It is difficult to make a logical case for the notion that persons with high MC scores would underreport using any alcohol during the past year to present a favorable image to the interviewer, unless we start by assuming that such respondents think that abstinence is desirable behavior. Once we make that assumption, we would also assume that having such a norm about drinking would affect real drinking behavior.

It is somewhat easier to assume that persons may feel that enjoying the effects of alcohol may be contrary to the Puritan tradition. It is one thing to have an occasional sociable drink or a little port for your digestion, but it is quite another thing to feel high or intoxicated from alcoholic beverages. If we look at our survey data, we see that only 39 percent of the persons who drank during the year prior to the survey report ever having been intoxicated during that time (see Table 38). Thus, we postulate a norm of moderation, which limits the amount of alcohol most people drink and which probably also limits the perception (or recollection) of having been somewhat intoxicated. We further assume that some persons would falsely disclaim intoxication to an interviewer. However, since we know that MC scores are widely reflected in behavior (including behavior that has no normative implications), we assume that they will also be reflected in real behavior in this area; we expect that those persons with high MC scores who do drink are less likely to become intoxicated than persons with lower scores.

Although the decriminalization of marijuana has proceeded since the time of the survey, reports of having tried marijuana were reports of illegal behavior. In addition to the illegal aspect of marijuana use, any drug use is viewed as dangerous (and probably immoral) by segments of the population. In a 1977 Gallup survey, more than one half of the respondents reported that they thought marijuana was physically harmful, addictive, and led to the use of hard drugs. In our sample, only 22 percent of the respondents reported ever having tried marijuana. Once again, it seems reasonable to assume that a substantial proportion of the population views the use of marijuana as contranormative. Although some subgroups of the population do not hold this norm, there are some people who probably would falsely claim not to have tried marijuana in response

Table 38. MC Scores for Persons Reporting Intoxication and Marijuana Use

	Number	*Score*[a]	*Score Adjusted for Age*[a]
Number of Times Intoxicated Past Year			
Never	560	.34	.20
Less Than Once a Month	274	−.42	−.21
Once a Month or More	79	−.96	−.69
Mean = 5.68	N = 913	Eta = .23	Beta = .14
Marijuana Use (Ever)			
No	911	.31	.20
Yes	253	−1.10	−.72
Mean = 5.90	N = 1164	Eta = .29	Beta = .19

[a]Expressed as deviations from the mean.

to a survey question. We expect that persons with high MC scores would be less likely to try marijuana than persons with lower scores.

The counterinterpretation, which would be made by those who see MC scores as measures of a tendency to manipulate survey responses, is obvious. They would assume that persons with high scores would become intoxicated or try marijuana as often as persons with lower scores and that they simply underreport their own behavior. Further, since these two behaviors are more clearly contranormative than simply using alcohol, persons accepting the response-bias interpretation would expect stronger negative correlations between scores and marijuana use and intoxication than between scores and alcohol use.

The correlations in our data do not support this expectation. There are negative correlations between MC scores and having been intoxicated ($-.257$); among those who drank during the past year ($N = 919$), the correlation is $-.226$; controlling for age reduces this correlation to $-.109$. The correlation between MC scores and having tried marijuana is $-.295$. These correlations are of the same general magnitude as the correlation with having drunk any alcohol during the year before the survey ($-.279$) and are only slightly larger than the correlation with general sociability ($-.212$). If we simply control for age, the three correlations are reduced to $-.110$ between scores and sociability, $-.152$ between scores and having tried marijuana, and $-.163$ between scores and drinking alcohol.

If we look at the zero order correlations between intoxication and marijuana use and our independent variables, we see that they are virtually identical, with two exceptions. First, as one would expect, there is a somewhat stronger correlation between marijuana use and age ($-.424$) than there is between intoxication and age ($-.354$). Second, the correlation between having been intoxicated and rural residence is negligible ($-.050$), but the correlation between rural residence and marijuana use is stronger ($-.170$). Older people retain older norms about marijuana use, and people in rural areas may also retain such norms. Marijuana is also less readily available to older persons than it is to the young, and it may be less readily available in some rural areas. In Table 38, we see the average MC scores associated with having been intoxicated and having used marijuana. Even when we control for age, there are strong persistent relationships between MC scores and reports of these behaviors.

Some Comments on Age, Cohort, and Behavior

Since the correlations with age are so strong ($-.364$ with having been intoxicated and $-.424$ with having tried marijuana), we should perhaps explore what controlling for age means in this context. We think that a certain number of older persons are constrained from any drinking or to moderation in alcohol for health reasons; further, we have seen that older persons are less active and sociable than younger persons, and for that reason they may simply have fewer opportunities to drink or to become intoxicated. We see this as the aging effect and suppose that some younger persons who now occasionally drink and become intoxicated will not do so later in life.

We also imagine, however, that there is a cohort effect. Our older sample members were socialized before the cocktail was invented, lived through the prohibition era when alcohol was illegal and associated with criminal activities, and thus seem to us to be less likely to drink at all (or to allow themselves to become drunk if they do drink) than are younger members of our sample. Laws against drinking, and norms against drinking that allowed the laws to be enacted (if not enforced), are part of the life experience of older sample members. Somewhat younger persons in our sample did not have that life experience; neither did they experience widespread use of marijuana among their peers. These are the persons who may have been intoxicated but would not have tried marijuana. This, too, seems to be partly the effect of cohort experience. The youngest group in our sample came of age when marijuana was widely used and readily available to young people. This behavior was initially contranormative in the larger society but acceptable and comfortable for those under thirty. As our zero order correlations suggest, having been intoxicated and having tried marijuana are associated with many of the same social characteristics, except for age. We suggest that this difference may also be interpreted as a cohort effect.

We may derive some notion of the cohort effect (as opposed to the aging effect) by comparing A, B, and C in Table 39. Sample members who have never used any alcoholic beverages are six years older than the average sample member. This seems to us to indicate a cohort effect, since these abstainers can never be replaced by younger sample members. The aging effect seems visible when we

Table 39. Birth Year (± one standard deviation) of Persons Reporting Behaviors

1900 1905 1910 1915 1920 1925 1930 1935 1940 1945 1950 1955

Total Sample (Mean Age = 43)

A. Never Drank (Mean Age = 49, N = 107)

B. Drank But Not in Past Year (Mean Age = 55, N = 103)

C. Drank in Past Year (Mean Age = 41, N = 961)

D. Intoxicated in Past Year, Never Tried Marijuana (Mean Age = 38, N = 189)

E. Ever Tried Marijuana (Mean Age = 29, N = 253)

(Tried Marijuana Only; Mean Age = 31, N = 89)

(Intoxicated and Tried Marijuana; Mean Age = 28, N = 164)

F. High MC Scores (8–10) (Mean Age = 50, N = 249)

G. Medium MC Scores (5–7) (Mean Age = 43, N = 631)

H. Low MC Scores (0–4) (Mean Age = 35, N = 284)

Note: Data collected in summer 1975.

note that persons who have tried alcohol but have not drunk any in the past year are an average of six years older than the total abstainers and fourteen years older than the current drinkers. (There is probably also a cohort effect, since older persons may have tended to abstain and have drunk extremely infrequently throughout their lives.)

If we compare lines C and D, we see that persons who report having been intoxicated are slightly younger than the average drinkers in our sample. This difference may indicate a combination of moderation accompanying age and residual cohort effects—that is, a general tendency to moderation in the older cohort.

Marijuana use will probably persist as the current users age and may in time resemble line C (although we would have to add a line parallel to line B for persons who stop using marijuana for reasons of decreased sociability and impaired health, which accompany aging, as well as a tendency to greater moderation, which aging may produce).

We have also seen that age is strongly correlated with MC scores. In this context, age may be considered to be an indicator of the probability that people were brought up to believe in inflexible standards for behavior that are imposed from outside. They may conceive of traditional norms as inviolable and measure their own behavior in uncompromising terms. Important life experiences such as education or occupational experience may to some extent offset the effects of rigid child training. We do not have enough measures of current life situation or original family background to explore this matter in any depth.

We suspect, but cannot demonstrate, that the relation between MC scores and age is substantially a cohort effect. Older persons may have been brought up to obey the rules and then may have been only partially successful in transmitting their notions of obedience to their children in a changing social climate.

We have argued (starting from the manifest content of scale items) that MC scores represent a way of conceiving of and relating to norms. The 103 members of our sample (9 percent) who never tried alcohol certainly conceive of and relate to the norms about drinking behavior in terms of absolutes. They claim never to have tried an alcoholic beverage. Although it is possible that these people have an inviolable rule about their drinking behavior and flexible rules for all their other behavior, it is more likely that they have other absolute standards. If their life experiences have led them to think in terms of absolute abstinence from alcohol, those same life experiences may have led them to other absolutes. If we compare lines A and F in Table 39, we see that the historical environment of total abstainers is almost precisely the same as that of persons with high MC scores. Since, over time, sample members can only leave (not join) the total-abstainers category, we suggest that the six-year age difference between lifetime abstainers and average sample members is a conservative indication of cohort effect; the historical environment associated with abstinence no longer exists. For similar reasons, we think that high MC scores associated with age may be substantially a cohort effect.

We have seen that MC scores are inversely related to general activities ($-.218$), sociability ($-.212$), drinking ($-.279$), intoxication ($-.257$), and marijuana use ($-.275$). Simply controlling for age reduces the correlations to $-.07$ for activities, $-.11$ for sociability, $-.16$ for drinking, $-.13$ for intoxication, and $-.15$ for marijuana use. Those who view MC scores as indicators of response distortion could claim that the persistent negative correlations with drinking, intoxication, and marijuana use represent response bias. They could not account for the parallel negative correlations with general activities and sociability.

We consider MC scores to indicate personality traits that are associated with limited social environments and a wide range of behaviors. We expected that MC scores would be negatively related to all these measures, not because respondents are manipulating the image they present in the interview situation, but because persons with high scores have different life experiences and behave differently from persons with lower scores.

MC Scores and Cognitive Style

Since we argue that MC scores are related to personality traits as well as to a wide variety of real-world behaviors, it would be helpful if we could find evidence that the style of thinking of persons with high scores differed in some way other than either the MC scale itself or expressions of happiness and satisfaction. Both of these are positively related to MC scores, but one cannot know whether people are expressing their true feelings of happiness and satisfaction or whether their true feelings (known to them) are being disguised in reports during the survey interview. We tried to find evidence that could not be linked to a response-bias interpretation — evidence that could not be presumed by anyone to be related to problems of self-presentation during the survey interview.

We were able to look at one aspect of the data that seemed to us to be divorced from any possibility of manipulation by respondents in the interest of image-enhancement. After being asked the ten questions about feelings, respondents were asked to provide numerical estimates of the frequency of those feelings: "When you said that you felt particularly excited or interested in something (very often, pretty often, or not too often) about how many times a month did you mean?" The question was repeated for the number of times they felt bored. Of all the items in our data, these two seem to us most clearly reflections of style of thinking. Any differences in these answers associated with MC scores cannot reasonably be attributed to image-management.

In Table 40, we show the mean number given by respondents by MC score group. Although there was wide variety in the answers respondents provided (as indicated by the standard deviations), it is interesting to note the similarity across items: To persons with low MC scores, "very often" means about twenty-one times a month for both excitement and boredom; to persons with high scores, "very often" means about fifteen times. An almost identical pattern emerges twice from the chaos of answers.

Table 40. How Often Is Very Often?

MC Score	Excited			Bored		
	Mean	S.D.	Number[a]	Mean	S.D.	Number[a]
Low	22.79	21.22	57	20.03	10.72	29
Medium	16.72	14.07	126	17.06	15.11	50
High	15.22	9.82	64	14.40	10.02	20
	$F = 4.331$ (d.f. 2,244)			$F = 1.139$ (d.f. 2,96) n.s.		

[a] This table includes only persons who responded that they were excited or bored very often.

The correlation between MC scores and how often respondents meant when they said they had been excited or interested in something very often is $-.176$ ($p = .003$). If we look at the scattergram of this relationship, we see that there are twelve very high choices (in this case, more often than once a day). None of these were made by the sixty-four persons with high scores, four were made by the one hundred twenty-six persons with medium scores, and eight were made by the fifty-seven persons with low scores.

In a sense, this fits perfectly with earlier evidence. If persons participate in fewer general activities and less social life, we might expect that it would take fewer units of something for them to regard it as very often. If they have a low threshold for "very often," might they not have low thresholds for other extremes? When they report being completely satisfied, they may be honestly evaluating something that has a lower absolute level than would be required for persons with a lower MC score to make the same claim.

Conclusions

In reviewing our research, we find two of the results most compelling. First, the correlation between MC scores and marital status, which suggests to us pervasive, real-world differences in the way persons with high and low MC scores behave and relate to other people. Second, the cognitive differences between persons with high and low scores seem most clearly demonstrated by the lower frequency assigned to "very often" by persons with high scores. This lower frequency conforms perfectly to the limited participation in general activities and in social life already revealed in our analysis to be related to higher scores.

We do not mean to imply that there are no distortions in survey data based on the respondent's need to convey a particular image to the interviewer or to any relative stranger to whom he or she relates. We simply suggest that one method of attempting to identify the persons most prone to such distortion—the Marlowe-Crowne scale—does not seem effective to this end. The variance associated with high MC scores in survey data should be considered part of the real variance in the data. The scale was introduced into our own research in an attempt to assess the contribution of the need for approval (social desirability) to the error variance in our data. We concluded that the variance associated with the MC scale was part of the real variance in our data. In other chapters, we have suggested solutions to response-bias problems; we regret that we must in this case remove a solution that has been used in several major research projects. The Marlowe-Crowne scale is an extremely interesting variable, but its utility does not lie in the identification of persons in a survey sample who are most likely to distort their responses to survey questions.

Chapter Seven

Consequences of Informed Consent on Response Rate and Quality

Our age, as Bernard Barber (1973) put it, is the "age of civil rights"; it is an age of increasing concern for the protection of individual rights against institutional encroachment and abuse. One area of concern is that of research involving human subjects— primarily, but not exclusively, biomedical research—and one issue that has gained prominence within that area is the issue of informed

Note: Adapted from Eleanor Singer, "Informed Consent," *American Sociological Review,* April 1978, *43,* 144–161.

consent. That issue has been sharpened by existing and proposed regulations designed to protect the rights of human subjects.

Among scientists, debate over these regulations has been conducted, largely without benefit of empirical evidence, between those who champion the new rules on ethical grounds (for example, Gray, 1975; Warwick, 1975) and those who oppose them in the belief that they will destroy the possibility of doing needed research. The present study was designed to provide evidence bearing on this issue in social survey research.

Design of the Study

The study reported in this chapter was conducted in 1976 to investigate the effects of three factors that, together, may be said to constitute informed consent procedures in face-to-face interviews with a random sample of the adult population.

The first of these factors was the amount of information given to respondents ahead of time about the content of the interview. Conventional survey wisdom advocates keeping the introduction short, so as not to lose the respondent's interest or attention; some evidence from experiments with mail questionnaires suggests that a general explanation of purpose is preferable to a more detailed one, which may antagonize some respondents (Blumberg, Fuller, and Hare, 1974); and the advice in the most recent edition of the *Handbook of Social Psychology*, as in earlier editions, is to keep subjects in laboratory experiments ignorant of the true purpose of the research (Aronson and Carlsmith, 1968).

At the same time, some investigators support fuller disclosure of research purposes to respondents. Jourard (1964, 1968) and Jourard and Friedman (1970), for example, have argued that the most powerful determinant of self-disclosure by experimental subjects is self-disclosure on the part of the experimenter. Although these methods do not appear to be readily adaptable to the usual laboratory situation, they may have more direct implications for survey research. If Jourard and Friedman are correct, then full disclosure of the purpose of a survey—although not necessarily of specific hypotheses—may actually result in a higher response rate and less response distortion than attempts at deception. Some support for this derives from a study of telephone household screening

(Hauck and Cox, 1974). In that study, refusals were reduced after respondents were given a more nearly complete and accurate description of the purpose of the study.

Accordingly, we constructed two descriptions of the content of the interview to be read to respondents ahead of time. Half the respondents were given a brief, vague description of the survey as a study of leisure time and the way people are feeling. The other half were given a fuller description of the interview, which contained a large number of questions generally considered sensitive. These respondents were told:

> We're conducting a national survey about how people are feeling in general and about the kinds of activities people do in their leisure time—that is, their spare time when they are not working. There are questions about your moods, and about the time you spend watching television or going to sports events, about your social activities, and some about your use of alcoholic drinks. We also ask a few questions about sex.

Aside from being shorter, the short introduction was, essentially, a "deceit" condition. Though the deceit was mild, the information given to the respondent ahead of time was not consistent with the relatively heavy emphasis on drinking, sex, and mental health in the interview. Taking into account all the cross-pressures reviewed above, we expected no significant differences in initial refusal between information conditions, but more accurate reporting (more admission of "undesirable" behavior) once the respondent had agreed to participate.

The second factor that was experimentally varied in the study was the assurance of confidentiality given to respondents. It has become increasingly clear that, although some research organizations, such as NORC, routinely promise to protect the confidentiality of respondent replies, such guarantees ordinarily have no legal standing; the relation between researcher and respondent is not recognized as privileged. If records are subpoenaed, there is ultimately nothing, short of going to jail, that the researcher can do to redeem the promise of confidentiality made to respondents. If there is no need to identify respondents for administrative purposes or follow-up studies, the problem of confidentiality can sometimes be handled by destroying overtly identifying information. But in small and specialized populations, even this strategy will not prevent the identification of the respondent from other bits of information routinely punched on IBM cards (see Nejelski, 1976).

Unlike other arguments for informed consent, which are advanced on ethical grounds only, the argument for confidentiality is advanced on pragmatic grounds as well. That is, not only is breach of confidentiality a *risk* to which respondents are exposed by virtue of participating in the survey, but it has also been argued that respondents will not give valid information without the promise that the confidentiality of their replies will be maintained.

Although no prior research on the effects of confidentiality existed when this study was designed, research on the closely related factor of anonymity suggests that *response rates* are not much affected either by the presence or absence of an identifying code or by the form of identification used (Erdos and Regir, 1977; Mitchell, 1939). Aside from its effect on response rates, lack of anonymity has frequently been considered a potential source of *bias* in mail surveys. Fuller (1974), however, concluded from her review of the literature that the risk of significant bias was relatively small. Although a few researchers have found some systematic bias, others have not, even when the information was somewhat sensitive (for example, see Ash and Abramson, 1952; Fischer, 1946; King, 1970; Wildman, 1977).

To investigate the effects of variations on confidentiality, one third of the respondents in the present study were told nothing at all about the confidentiality of their replies; one third were given an absolute assurance of confidentiality ("Of course, your answers will remain completely confidential"); and one third were given a qualified assurance of confidentiality ("Of course, we will do our best to protect the confidentiality of your answers, except as required by law").

The final factor that was varied in the study was whether or not a signature was required to document consent and, if so, whether the request for a signature came before or after the interview. It is generally assumed that requiring a signature to document consent lowers response rates, although the research on anonymity, which also bears indirectly on this problem, suggests that this effect may well be small. Deferring a signature until after the interview has been completed has several potential advantages: (1) in some sense, truly "informed" consent can only be given after the respondent has heard the actual questions; (2) responses, as distinct from response rate, will be unaffected by a request for a signature at the end of the interview; (3) response rate may be protected to some extent if the respondent, having invested time in giving the interview, is reluctant to see it wasted by refusing to sign the consent form.

Aside from these three factors, which can represent different levels of risk or cost to respondents, certain elements of the introduction were kept constant. All respondents were told that the study was being done by the National Opinion Research Center; that the interview would take about half an hour; that they would then be asked to fill out a short, self-administered form; that participation was voluntary; and that they could refuse questions within the interview. Every introduction also included a plea for honesty of response if the person decided to participate.

The three factors described above were combined in a 2 × 3 × 3 factorial design, yielding eighteen different introductions to respondents. These introductions were stapled to the household enumeration folders assigned to each interviewer, along with instructions for answering questions and objections, also specifically tailored to each version of the introduction. Interviewers were instructed to read the introduction in its entirety to the selected respondent and to give standardized replies to questions that might be raised about content, confidentiality, or signature.

A national probability sample of 2,084, drawn within fifty primary sampling units of NORC's master sample, was used for the study. Interviewers were required to list all household members and to select the appropriate respondent according to a sampling table. Each sample line (household) had been assigned a randomly selected experimental treatment in the central office. Every interviewer was assigned thirty-one sample lines, and every interviewer's assignment included all eighteen versions of the introduction.

The interview schedule was substantially the same as that used a year earlier and described in Chapter Two. The questionnaire was designed to permit investigation of the effect of informed consent procedures on different types of questions—sensitive and nonsensitive survey-specific and general questions about attitudes and behavior.

Also measured in the study were respondents' reactions to the interview, ascertained by means of a self-administered questionnaire, filled out immediately following the interview and handed to the interviewer in a sealed envelope, and interviewers' expectations about the reactions to the study, assessed just prior to and after the completion of fieldwork. After all interviewing had been completed, each respondent was sent a letter thanking him or her for participating, explaining that the study had had a methodological as well as a substantive purpose, and briefly describing that purpose.

With one exception, only experienced NORC interviewers—almost one third of whom had worked on the national study a year earlier—were used on this survey. They were trained in the special experimental procedures for the study through a combination of written materials, group telephone briefings by area supervisors, and specially developed training exercises that had to be completed before interviewing could begin. Interviews were edited in the New York office, and 20 percent of each interviewer's cases were validated.

Interviewers were told about the methodological purposes of the study but not about any specific hypotheses, and they were urged to keep an open mind about the effects of the experimental variables. Those who felt seriously uncomfortable with either the substantive or the methodological aspects of the study were asked not to take on this particular assignment; about five withdrew for this reason.

Several facts give us confidence that the interviewers followed the procedures specified. First, the two variations in the description of content had been tried earlier, in the 1975 study, with essentially the same results as those reported here. Second, evidence that the respondent was asked to sign the consent form is provided by the forms themselves, unless we assume that interviewers forged some signatures. No such evidence is available for confidentiality. However, we assume that distortions with respect to this variable, if they occurred, would have been in the direction of promising confidentiality to those respondents who should not have received such an assurance. Therefore, we will be on safe grounds if we treat the findings on confidentiality as *minimal* effects.

This chapter discusses the effect of each of the three experimental variables on three different types of outcomes: overall response rate to the survey, response rates to individual questions, and response quality.

Effects on Overall Response Rate

The overall response rate to the questionnaire was 67 percent; 87 percent of all households assigned, minus only those that were vacant or were not dwelling units, were successfully screened, and 77 percent of those screened were actually interviewed. Chi squares computed on the distribution of the actual gross sample—that is, the number of assigned lines plus those picked up by interviewers at previously unlisted dwelling units, minus thirty-one lines lost when one segment was dropped without replacement because of a very large proportion of non-English-speaking residents—and on the distribution of all those whose households were successfully listed indicate that they do not depart significantly from a distribution assuming an equal number of cases in each cell. That is, there were no differential losses from the sample during screening.

Of the three experimental variables, only the request for a signature had a statistically significant effect on the probability of responding, as evaluated by analysis of variance; 71 percent of those not asked to sign were interviewed, compared with only 64 percent of those asked before and 65 percent of those asked after (see Table 41). Even so, it should be noted that the refusal was limited to the signature itself. Only a handful of respondents actually refused to be interviewed; the rest agreed to the interview but refused to sign the consent form or signed after the interview rather than before. None of the interactions among independent variables was significant. Because those respondents who refused to sign the consent form were actually interviewed, it is possible to examine the effects of content and confidentiality alone—that is, ignoring the effect of the signature variable altogether—by including those who refused to sign the consent form. The overall response rate, under these circumstances, is of course higher—71 percent versus 67 percent—but neither content nor confidentiality has an effect on response rate.

Since the data fit an additive model, it is also possible to estimate the cumulative effect of all three informed consent vari-

Table 41. The Effect of Variations in Information About Content, Assurance of Confidentiality, and Request for a Signature on the Probability of Responding to the Interview[a]

| Independent Variables | Deviations | | N |
	Unadjusted/Adjusted[b]	Eta/Partial Beta[c]	
Content			
Long	.01/.01		922
Short	−.01/−.01	.03/.03	933
Confidentiality			
No Mention	.01/.01		634
Qualified	−.01/−.01		603
Absolute	.00/.00	.01/.01	618
Signature			
Not Asked	.04/.04		625
Asked Before	−.03/−.03		608
Asked After	−.02/−.02	.07/.07[d]	622

[a]Mean = .67.

[b]Adjusted for the effects of the other two independent variables — for example, confidentiality and signature in the case of content.

[c]These partial correlation ratios, labeled *betas* here, can be viewed as standardized partial regression coefficients. See Nie and others (1975, p. 417).

[d]Significant at the .01 level.

ables by summing the adjusted deviations associated with the short content, absolute confidentiality, and no-signature conditions—in other words, the standard survey introduction—and contrasting them with the summed deviations for the long, qualified, and signature-before conditions. The estimated response rates are 70 percent and 64 percent, respectively. That is, the estimated response-rate cost associated with all three elements of informed consent is no greater than that associated with the request for a signature alone.

It can be argued that there is no way for the experimental variables to affect the response rate unless the interviewer has actually read the appropriate introduction, but this is not necessarily true. If the interviewers had misgivings about certain introductions, they might have been less persistent in attempting to locate a respondent or less effective in obtaining an interview. Or, respondents might have asked questions about some of the experimental variables and declined to be interviewed on the basis of the responses they were given. Accordingly, we asked interviewers to indicate how much of the introduction had been read to each person who refused to be interviewed. Overwhelmingly—65 percent of the time—they reported that the refusal occurred before any part of the introduction had been read. The implications of this are considered later. Nevertheless, it was possible to examine refusals by experimental condition among those respondents who had heard the relevant portion of the introduction. For example, to examine the effect of information about content on refusals, we included all those to whom the interviewer had read at least that section of the introduction. To examine the effect of confidentiality, we included all those who had heard that portion of the introduction, and so on. We assumed that, as specified, the entire introduction had been read to all respondents who had been interviewed.

Table 42 shows the relation between experimental treatment and refusal for those to whom the relevant portions of the introduc-

Table 42. Refusal by Experimental Treatment Among Those Who Heard Relevant Portion of Introduction

Experimental Variable	Percentage Who Refused		Chi Square
Content			
Long	5		
		(693)[a]	
Short	4		
		(688)	1.68; n.s.
Confidentiality			
No Mention	4		
		(475)	
Qualified	3		
		(443)	
Absolute	3		
		(444)	0.61; n.s.
Signature			
Not Asked	0		
		(446)	
Asked Before	11		
		(443)	
Asked After	7		
		(439)	48.49; p <.01

[a]Numbers shown include only potential respondents who heard the relevant portion of the introduction.

tion had been read. That table confirms the conclusion drawn on the basis of the earlier analysis—namely, that only the request for a signature has a discernible effect on overall response.

Effects on Response Rates to Individual Questions

Although the interview schedule included many questions ordinarily considered sensitive or threatening, the rate of nonresponse to individual items was very low. Only two questions elicited a total nonresponse rate—that is, "no answer," "don't know," and "not asked"—of 10 percent or more: a question about income (11 percent nonresponse) and one about masturbation (10 percent nonresponse). Most items had nonresponse rates below 2 percent, and we did not examine the effect of the experimental variables on these. We did, however, examine all questions with a total nonresponse rate of more than 3 percent. All these questions asked about some item of behavior; none of the attitude questions elicited a nonresponse rate as high as 3 percent.

The results of this analysis are quickly summarized (for details, see Tables 43, 44, and 45). The amount of information given respondents ahead of time has no statistically significant or consistent effects on nonresponse to individual questions; in only one of twelve comparisons do differences in nonresponse exceed three percentage points.

The assurance of confidentiality, in contrast, does appear to affect the rate of nonresponse to individual questions. With one exception, respondents who were told that their answers would remain completely confidential had the lowest nonresponse rate of any of the three groups. In five of the twelve comparisons, these differences were statistically significant.

The final variable whose effect on item nonresponse we examined was the request for a signature and its timing. Since the present survey was an experiment rather than a study that actually required informed consent, we conducted interviews with those who refused to sign, coding their refusal. We are therefore able to compare the responses given to individual questions by those who agreed to sign and those who refused. An alternative method of analysis involves summing the number of nonresponses to all four items asked of the total sample and then comparing this index of

Table 43. Nonresponse[a] to Sensitive[b] Questions, by Information Condition

| Question | Percent Nonresponse | | |
	Long Introduction	Short Introduction	Significance[c]
Ever Smoked Marijuana Three Times per Week or More?[d]	4.7 (149)	9.3 (161)	n.s.
Number of Pipes, Joints Smoked per Time?[e]	4.7 (149)	6.2 (161)	n.s.
Engaged in Petting or Kissing Past Month?	7.3 (658)	5.3 (663)	n.s.
How Often?[d]	7.5 (465)	8.8 (445)	n.s.
Petting or Kissing Past 24 Hours?[d]	2.8 (465)	4.7 (445)	n.s.
Intercourse Past Month?	9.9 (658)	7.8 (663)	n.s.
How Often?[d]	11.3 (407)	8.7 (393)	n.s.
Intercourse Past 24 Hours?[d]	6.1 (407)	3.3 (393)	n.s.
Masturbation Past Month?	12.5 (658)	9.7 (663)	n.s.
How Often?[d]	7.0 (57)	8.3 (36)	n.s.
Masturbation Past 24 Hours?[d]	5.3 (57)	5.6 (36)	n.s.
Earned Income Past Year?	10.5 (658)	10.1 (663)	n.s.

[a]Nonresponse includes refusal, "don't know," and not asked.

[b]All questions on which more than 3 percent of responses were coded as missing data are included in this table. With one exception, they come from the "sensitive, survey-specific, factual" question category. The exception is the question on income, which is general rather than survey-specific.

[c]Significance levels are based on chi square.

[d]For these questions, we give the conditional probability of refusing to answer, among those who answered the filter question.

[e]On this particular question, sixteen of the seventeen missing responses are attributable to interviewer omissions rather than respondent refusals.

Table 44. Nonresponse[a] to Sensitive[b] Questions, by Confidentiality Condition

Question	Percent Nonresponse				Significance Level[c]
	No Mention of Confidentiality	Qualified Confidentiality	Absolute Confidentiality		
Ever Smoked Marijuana Three Times per Week or More?[d]	7.5 (120)	10.6 (94)	3.1 (96)		n.s.
Number of Pipes, Joints Smoked per Time?[e]	5.0 (120)	9.6 (94)	2.1 (96)		n.s.
Engaged in Petting or Kissing Past Month?	8.5 (457)	6.0 (430)	4.1 (434)		<.05
How Often?[d]	7.0 (315)	10.0 (289)	7.5 (306)		n.s.
Petting or Kissing Past 24 Hours?[d]	4.4 (315)	4.2 (289)	2.6 (306)		n.s.
Intercourse Past Month?	10.7 (457)	9.5 (430)	6.2 (434)		=.05
How Often?[d]	10.3 (271)	11.7 (257)	8.1 (272)		n.s.
Intercourse Past 24 Hours?[d]	6.3 (271)	5.8 (257)	2.2 (272)		=.05
Masturbation Past Month?	14.2 (457)	10.7 (430)	8.1 (434)		<.05
How Often?[d]	6.3 (32)	11.5 (26)	5.7 (35)		n.s.

							Significance[c]
Masturbation Past 24 Hours?[d]	6.3	(32)	7.7	(26)	2.9	(35)	n.s.
Earned Income Past Year?	12.9	(457)	10.7	(430)	7.1	(434)	<.05

[a]Nonresponse includes refusal, "don't know," and not asked.
[b]All questions on which more than 3 percent of responses were coded as missing data are included in this table. With one exception, they come from the "sensitive, survey-specific, factual" question category. The exception is the question on income, which is general rather than survey-specific.
[c]Significance levels are based on chi square.
[d]For these questions, we give the conditional probability of refusing to answer, among those who answered the filter question.
[e]On this particular question, sixteen of the seventeen missing responses are attributable to interviewer omissions rather than respondent refusals.

Table 45. Nonresponse[a] to Sensitive[b] Questions, by Signature Condition

Question	Percent Nonresponse				
	Asked Before	Asked After	Not Asked	Refused	Significance[c]
Ever Smoked Marijuana Three Times per Week or More?[d]	8.7 (104)	7.1 (98)	5.9 (101)	0 (7)	n.s.
Number of Pipes, Joints Smoked per Time?[e]	5.8 (104)	5.1 (98)	5.9 (101)	0 (7)	n.s.
Engaged in Petting or Kissing Past Month?	4.8 (392)	6.9 (406)	4.9 (449)	18.9 (74)	<0.5
How Often?[d]	7.5 (266)	6.5 (276)	7.7 (323)	24.4 (45)	<.05
Petting or Kissing Past 24 Hours?[d]	2.3 (266)	3.3 (276)	5.3 (323)	4.4 (45)	n.s.
Intercourse Past Month?	6.1 (392)	8.9 (406)	8.2 (449)	27.0 (74)	<.05
How Often?[d]	9.0 (244)	9.7 (238)	10.1 (287)	19.4 (31)	n.s.
Intercourse Past 24 Hours?[d]	3.7 (244)	5.0 (238)	4.5 (287)	12.9 (31)	n.s.
Masturbation Past Month?	8.2 (392)	11.6 (406)	10.2 (449)	28.4 (74)	<.05
How Often?[d]	0 (24)	12.9 (31)	8.6 (35)	0 (3)	n.s.

Masturbation Past 24 Hours?[d]	0	(24)	9.7	(31)	5.7	(35)	0	(3)	n.s.
Earned Income Past Year?	9.4	(392)	9.4	(406)	10.0	(449)	21.6	(74)	<.05

[a] Nonresponse includes refusal, "don't know," and not asked.

[b] All questions on which more than 3 percent of responses were coded as missing data are included in this table. With one exception, they come from the "sensitive, survey-specific, factual" question category. The exception is the question on income, which is general rather than survey-specific.

[c] Significance levels are based on chi square.

[d] For these questions, we give the conditional probability of refusing to answer, among those who answered the filter question.

[e] On this particular question, sixteen of the seventeen missing responses are attributable to interviewer omissions rather than respondent refusals.

nonresponse across experimental conditions. (Since the remaining questions are contingent on the others, they cannot be included in the index.) The data are shown in Table 46 and lead to the same conclusions reported previously.

As it turns out, the biggest differences in nonresponse are between those who refused to sign the consent form and those who either signed or were not asked to sign. Differences in nonresponse

Table 46. Variations in Nonresponse[a], by Experimental Condition

Experimental Conditions	Percentage with No Nonresponse to Any of Four Items		Mean Number of Nonresponses, Among Those with Any	
Content				
Long	81		2.08	
		(659)		(127)
Short	82		1.85	
		(662)		(118)
Significance of Difference[b]	$p = .47$		$p > .10$	
Confidentiality				
No Mention	77		2.04	
		(457)		(104)
Qualified	81		1.94	
		(430)		(82)
Absolute	87		1.88	
Significance		(434)		(59)
of Difference[b]	$p < .01$		$p \, (F) = .67$	
Signature				
Before	85		1.95	
		(392)		(58)
After	81		1.94	
		(406)		(77)
Not Asked	82		1.83	
		(449)		(82)
Refused	62		2.54	
		(74)		(28)
Significance of Difference[b,c]	$p < .01$		$p \, (F) = .05$	

[a] Based on an index of the four items with a nonresponse rate greater than 3 percent.
[b] Based on chi square for proportions and t-tests or one-way analysis of variance for means.
[c] When those who refused to sign are excluded from the analysis, the difference among conditions is not significant.

between the latter groups are very small—with one exception, two percentage points or less. Those who were asked to sign before the interview and agreed to do so were least likely to refuse to answer questions thereafter. However, those asked for a signature before-hand were more likely to refuse to sign at all; 10 percent of those asked to sign the consent form before the interview refused, as compared with 7 percent of those asked to sign afterwards. Among those who did sign the consent form, there were no differences in reluctance, as noted by interviewers at the conclusion of the inter-view; 87 percent of those who signed after the interview were judged not to have been reluctant at all, 12 percent were somewhat reluc-tant, and 1 percent were very reluctant. Among those who signed before, the corresponding percentages were 88, 11, and 1.

It would appear, in other words, that refusing to answer sensitive questions within the interview schedule serves the same purpose as refusing to sign a consent form. Since people are free to refuse particular questions and in fact seem to avail themselves of the opportunity to do so, the requirement of a signature to doc-ument consent may be unnecessarily burdensome, depriving researchers of information that people are otherwise perfectly willing to give.

The high item-nonresponse rate of those who had refused to sign the consent form led us to ask whether refusers are a dis-tinct group, inclined to say "no" to questions or requests they con-strue as sensitive, or whether perhaps asking respondents to sign a consent form ahead of time sensitizes them to the content of the interview, so that they are more likely to refuse to answer particu-lar questions during the interview itself. If the first hypothesis is true, there should be little, if any, difference in nonresponse to specific questions between those who refused to sign before and those who refused to sign afterwards. If the second hypothesis is true, high item-nonresponse rates should be characteristic only of those asked to sign a consent form before the interview.

The relevant data are shown in Table 47. Although the numbers on which the percentages in each cell are based are now very small, the figures support the interpretation that refusers are a distinct group. Eight of the twelve comparisons indicate that there are no differences in response tendencies to specific items between

Table 47. Nonresponse[a] to Sensitive[b] Questions Among Those Refusing
to Sign Before and Those Refusing to Sign After the Interview

	Percent Nonresponse	
Question	Refused to Sign Before	Refused to Sign After
Ever Smoked Marijuana Three Times per Week or More?	0 (5)	0 (2)
Number of Pipes, Joints Smoked per Time?	0 (5)	0 (2)
Engaged in Petting or Kissing Past Month?	13.6 (44)	26.7 (30)
How Often?	23.3 (30)	
Petting or Kissing Past 24 Hours?	6.7 (30)	0 (15)
Intercourse Past Month?	27.3 (44)	26.7 (30)
How Often?	12.5 (16)	26.7 (15)
Intercourse Past 24 Hours?	6.3 (16)	20.0 (15)
Masturbation Past Month?	27.3 (44)	30.0 (30)
How Often?	0 (2)	0 (1)
Masturbation Past 24 Hours?	0 (2)	0 (1)
Earned Income Past Year?	13.6 (44)	33.3 (30)

[a] Nonresponse includes refusal, "don't know," and not asked.
[b] All questions on which more than 3 percent of responses were coded as missing data are included in this table.

those who refused to sign before and those who refused to sign afterwards; the four that do indicate such a difference invariably produce a larger nonresponse tendency for the group refusing to sign the consent form after the interview. In other words, rather than the request for a signature sensitizing people to the content of the interview, it appears to be true that those who reacted negatively to some of the questions subsequently refused to sign the

Table 48. Effect of Demographic Characteristics on Refusal to Sign Consent Form

Demographic Characteristic	Percentage of All Those Asked to Sign Who Refused
Race	
White	8.7
	(807)
Black	5.6
	(54)
Sex	
Male	8.6
	(349)
Female	8.4
	(523)
Age	
18–25	2.6
	(156)
26–35	7.7
	(207)
36–45	9.8
	(123)
46–55	7.1
	(127)
56–65	11.3
	(133)
65 +	14.3
	(126)
Education	
11 Years or Less	11.6
	(275)
12 Years	6.9
	(331)
13–15 Years	5.7
	(140)
16 Years or More	8.9
	(124)

consent form. For the most part, however, signing the consent form appears to function simply as another sensitive question, so that those who refuse the questions refuse to sign, and vice versa.

Age, sex, race, and number of years of school were examined as potential predictors of refusal to sign the consent form. Table 48 indicates that men and women were equally likely to refuse, and that differences between black and white respondents were small. The relation between education and refusal may be nonmonotonic, with those respondents having less than a high school education and those with a college degree or more being more likely to refuse than intermediate groups; the highest refusal rate occurred among those with the least education.

The strongest relationship, however, is between refusal and age. With one reversal, as age increases, so does refusal to sign the consent form, and when all four variables were entered simultaneously into a regression equation, only age retained a significant effect. However, all four together account for less than 1 percent of the variance in refusal.

Effects on Quality of Response

Previous research has indicated that for sensitive or threatening questions, more reporting is better reporting. (See references in Chapters One and Two.) In contrast, for attitudes and behaviors that are positively valued in a society—for example, voting, owning a library card, and holding liberal racial views—less reporting may be considered better reporting. Accordingly, we can ask two questions of the data from the present study: Do informed consent procedures have any significant or consistent effects on responses? If so, do they make for better reporting or worse?

As in the analysis of response rate to the questionnaire as a whole, the method of analysis used is multiple classification analysis, which is particularly well suited to the categorical form of the independent variables. The assumption of an additive model, on which multiple classification analysis is based, is supported by the fact that fewer than one in twenty of the two-way interactions among independent variables reach statistical significance. In examining the effect of each independent variable, we control not only for the other two but also for age, sex, and education, which influence many of the attitudes and behaviors in question.

For the analysis of response quality, we selected samples of nonsensitive attitude and behavioral questions, but we have included virtually every question, whether about attitudes or behavior, that could be construed as sensitive. The effects of all three independent variables are summarized in Table 49.

Table 49. Responses to Different Types of Questions as a Function of Content, Confidentiality, and Request for Signature[a]

	Content	Confidentiality	Signature
Effect on Sensitive, General Attitude Questions			
Social Desirability Scale	S[b]	N[c]	B[d]
Satisfaction with Financial Situation	S	N	B
Effect on Nonsensitive, General Attitude Questions			
Satisfaction with House	L	Q	=
Satisfaction with Neighborhood	S	Q[e]	B
Effect on Sensitive, Survey-Specific Attitude Questions			
Positive Affect Scale	=	N[e]	B
Negative Affect Scale	S[e]	C	A
22-Item Scale	S[e]	Q	N
Reported Happiness	S[e]	Q	A
Effect on Nonsensitive, Survey-Specific Attitude Questions			
Importance of Leisure	L	N	B
Satisfaction with Leisure	S	N	A
Effect on Sensitive, General Factual Questions			
Number of Sources of Income	L	C	B
Amount of Earned Income	L[e]	Q	A
Effect on Nonsensitive, General Factual Questions			
Number of Years of School	S	C	N
Probability of Giving Occupation as Professional or Managerial	S	N[e]	=

[a]Respondents who refused to sign the consent form are excluded from the analysis.

[b]L means that respondents given the long introduction produce better quality (that is, higher reporting levels); S means those given the short introduction give better responses; an equal sign means there are no differences.

[c]C means that those given an absolute assurance of confidentiality give the best responses; N means that those to whom confidentiality is not mentioned do; Q means that respondents in the qualified confidentiality condition give the best responses. An equal sign means there is a tie between respondents in the absolute and one of the other conditions.

[d]B means those asked to sign before the interview give the best responses; A means those asked afterward do; N means that those not asked for a signature produce the best responses. An equal sign means there is a tie between two conditions — "not asked" and "after" on probability of bowling and of masturbation in past month, "before" and "after" on the remaining items.

[e]p (F) $<$ .05.

Table 49. Responses to Different Types of Questions as a Function of Content, Confidentiality, and Request for Signature[a] (continued)

	Content	Confidentiality	Signature
Effect on Nonsensitive, Survey-Specific Factual Questions			
Probability of Going to a Restaurant	=	=	N
Probability of Bowling	L	=	=
Probability of Swimming	S	C	A
Frequency of Giving a Party	L	Q	A
Frequency of Being with Relatives	L	C	B
Effect on Sensitive, Survey-Specific Factual Questions			
Probability of Petting or Kissing Past Month	L	C	N
Petting Frequency	S	C	A
Petting Past 24 Hours	S	Q	A
Probability of Intercourse Past Month	=	C	N
Frequency of Intercourse	S	C	A
Intercourse Past 24 Hours	S	=	A[e]
Probability of Masturbation Past Month	L[e]	C	=
Frequency of Masturbation	L	C	A
Probability of Smoking Marijuana	S	N	=
Conditional Probability of Smoking Marijuana Past Year	L	C	B
Conditional Probability of Smoking Marijuana Three Times per Week or More	L	N	B[e]
Number of Pipes, Joints Smoked per Time	L[e]	N	B
Number of Close Friends Who Smoke	S	N	A[e]
Number of Times Drunk last Year	L	N	A
Number of Friends Drunk last Year	S	N	B[e]
Probability of Drinking Liquor	S	N	B

Table 49. Responses to Different Types of Questions as a Function of Content, Confidentiality, and Request for Signature[a] (continued)

	Content	Confidentiality	Signature
Conditional Probability of Drinking Past Year	S	Q	A
Frequency of Drinking	S	C	A
Number of Drinks per Time	L	C	N
Probability of Drinking Beer	S	=	N
Conditional Probability of Drinking Beer	S	Q	A
Frequency of Drinking Beer	L	N	A
Number of Beers per Time	L	Q	A[e]
Gambling Scale Score	S	N	A

The evidence for the effect of information about content on response quality is mixed. Only five comparisons (out of forty-three) between experimental conditions are statistically significant. On two sensitive, survey-specific attitude items, the vague, brief introduction results in better response quality (more reported negative affect, less reported happiness). On three behavioral items (income, masturbation, number of pipes or joints of marijuana smoked), the long introduction results in higher estimates than the short. Even if one chooses to ignore statistical significance and to look instead at consistency of response, no clear pattern is discernible.

Variations in confidentiality produce only three statistically significant differences in response quality—one in the category of nonsensitive general attitude questions, one in the category of sensitive survey-specific attitude questions, and one in the category of nonsensitive general factual questions. In two of these comparisons, the condition in which no mention is made of confidentiality produces the best data (lower scores on the Bradburn Positive Affect Scale, less likelihood of giving one's occupation as professional or managerial); in the third, the "qualified" confidentiality condition produces the best data (less reported satisfaction with the neighborhood).

These three instances do not speak compellingly for or against any confidentiality condition, nor is any consistent pattern of response apparent. Thus, although confidentiality affects non-response to individual questions, it does not appear to have any additional effect on response quality if the respondent decides to answer the question.

As in the case of content and confidentiality, very few of the comparisons involving the signature variable reach statistical significance; the five that do, however, all involve sensitive survey-specific behavioral questions, and all of them indicate that respondents who sign the consent form, either before or after the interview, report higher frequencies of such behavior than respondents who are not asked to sign.

One reason for this result is that respondents who *refused* to sign the consent form, and who therefore are properly excluded from the analysis, tend to give the lowest estimates of sensitive behavior. In other words, people who sign the consent form produce better data than those not asked to sign, because those who report the lowest frequencies of sensitive behavior also refuse to sign the consent form and are therefore excluded from the analysis. However, the estimates of threatening behavior given by those who sign the consent form *after* the interview tend to be higher than those given by respondents who sign before. Since the latter group shows little difference from the group not asked to sign at all, even though the request for a signature screens out some underestimators, we conclude that asking for a signature before the interview has a sensitization effect—respondents are more likely to underestimate socially undesirable behavior if they are asked to sign the consent form before the interview than if they are not asked to sign at all, or if they are asked to sign afterwards.

So far, we have examined response tendencies produced by the three independent variables considered one at a time and have concluded that these are for the most part small. But ethical considerations and statutory requirements call for incorporating not one but at least two and perhaps all three variables into survey introductions to secure the informed consent of the respondent. What, then, is the cumulative effect on response quality of all three independent variables examined in this study?

One approach to answering this question is to contrast the two extreme conditions already described. One is the "standard" survey introduction, in which the respondent is ordinarily given only vague, general information about the content of the interview, is assured that his or her replies will be held in strict confidence, and is not asked to sign a consent form. The other is the condition that, it might be argued, most nearly assures the informed consent of survey respondents—it provides detailed information about the content of the interview, qualifies the assurance of confidentiality, and asks the respondent to document his or her understanding and agreement by signing a consent form before being interviewed. Under these contrasting conditions, what effects on response tendencies can be discerned?

To answer this question, we examined responses in the two experimental conditions (out of eighteen) that represent the two sets of contrasting conditions. Because the numbers of cases are now very small (eighty-one in the "standard" and sixty-six in the "informed consent" condition), we did not attempt to control for other variables. Some five differences between the two conditions are statistically significant. Of these, three indicate better responses on the part of those in the informed consent condition, although only one of the three is a response to a sensitive item.

If we look at the pattern of responses rather than at statistical significance, the standard introduction appears to yield better data on sensitive survey-specific attitude questions, whereas the introduction involving informed consent yields better data on fourteen of twenty sensitive behavioral items on which any difference is discernible. Because of the absence of controls for age, sex, and education, we do not wish to overemphasize these findings. It should be emphasized once again, however, that both conclusions rely only on the pattern of responses and that most differences between experimental conditions are too small to reach statistical significance.

Conclusions

This study was designed to provide information to guide policy. What are the implications of its findings?

Four of those findings deserve emphasis. First, of the three experimental variables—content, confidentiality, and signature—only the request for a signature affects the response rate to the questionnaire as a whole. About 8 percent of those asked to sign a consent form refuse to do so, although they are willing to be interviewed.

Second, those who refuse to sign a consent form are also much more likely to refuse to answer individual questions within the interview and to provide poorer data when they do answer. Thus, paradoxically, the estimates obtained from a survey on sensitive topics may be improved if those who refuse to sign are excluded from the sample. However, this is true only for those asked to sign after the interview. For those asked to sign before, the request appears to have a sensitization effect, so that these respondents are more likely to underestimate socially undesirable behavior than if they had not been asked to sign at all or if they had been asked to sign afterwards.

Since the request for a signature appears to function largely as another sensitive question, the requirement that researchers obtain a signature to document consent seems unnecessarily burdensome. The same protection is afforded respondents by the right to refuse the interview or to refuse to answer particular questions within the interview. However, if a signature is required, it should be obtained after the interview rather than before, so as not to jeopardize the quality of the response.

The third major finding is that assuring respondents of absolute confidentiality has a small but significant and consistent effect on willingness to answer individual questions. Nonresponse rates for sensitive questions are consistently and sometimes significantly lower when people are told that their replies will be held in confidence, even though it was impossible to discern any significant effects of confidentiality on overall response rate or on response quality. If respondents can be assured of the confidentiality of their replies, response rates to sensitive questions will benefit. But such assurances must be meaningful; they cannot be given lightly. This means that government will have to accept greater restraints on access to information than it has yet indicated a willingness to accept; it also means more efforts by research organizations to maintain the confidentiality of research data within the organization itself.

Finally, since a more detailed, informative, and truthful introduction affects neither overall response rate nor responses to individual questions, there appears to be no reason to withhold such information from respondents.

All these findings, it should be emphasized, derive from one type of survey only. It is possible that certain types of questions asked of certain specialized categories of respondents might interact with the independent variables to produce results other than those reported here. For example, if welfare clients were asked about their income, refusals under several of the experimental conditions might be higher than those reported here; the same could be true if employees of a large corporation were asked about their drinking habits. One study cannot hope to answer all such questions; this one specifies what is likely to happen in a general population survey dealing with generally sensitive content.

The larger implications of the findings reported here are far from clear. One may optimistically conclude that none of the elements of informed consent, except the request for a signature, has sizable effects on the response rate to surveys or the quality of response and, therefore, that ethical imperatives do not conflict with practical considerations. Or, one may take the more pessimistic view that respondents simply do not attend to what they are told, deciding whether to participate or not on grounds entirely extraneous to those that are experimentally varied here. Two thirds of those who refused the interview, for example, had heard no part of the introduction whatsoever. In this more pessimistic view, the findings indicate only that the procedures used in this survey fail to ensure truly informed consent on the part of participants in social research.

Chapter Eight

Interviewing in the Presence of Others

It is generally considered good field practice not to have anyone other than the interviewer and respondent present during a face-to-face interview, and our experience is that interviewers are specifically instructed to question the respondent alone for surveys that ask socially sensitive questions. However, rules against interviewing respondents in the presence of others are not placed in field manuals, and interviewers are allowed to conduct an interview in the presence of a third party, if further efforts to secure privacy seem likely to lead to a refusal to be interviewed. As a result, almost every face-to-face household survey has some cases for which a third party was present.

There are good reasons to accept these cases. First, many surveys are not likely to be sensitive to the presence of third parties. Second, the biases incurred in eliminating interviews with third

Note: Prepared for this volume by Edward Blair.

parties present might very well be greater than the response effects caused by the third parties. The most common third-party scenarios described by our interviewers are the mother supervising her children—often too young to understand the survey topic—while she is being interviewed and the wife watching or listening while her husband is being interviewed. In most of these cases, the third party cannot be gotten out without incurring a refusal, and the failure to get these particular types of respondent could cause bias. It seems wiser to keep the case and to deal with the impact of the third party on response effects.

What is the impact of third parties on response effects? How often are third parties present, and what effect do they have? The only number available is a guess by Taietz (1962), unsupported by data, that third parties are present in 10 percent of the interviews conducted in surveys of the general population. The empirical literature on the effects of third parties when present is similarly scant, but it hints that response effects occur only when their potential is greatest. This chapter reports data that third parties are present in a much larger number of cases and have surprisingly small effects.

Third parties can be separated into two types—those brought in by the interviewer and not known to the respondent, and those present in the household and known to the respondent. The former group includes supervisors and, in a certain sense, tape recorders, which admit the possibility of the interview being replayed for any number of unknown third parties. We are not considering the effects of third parties in out-of-household locations.

Third parties brought in by the interviewers do not seem to influence responses. Bucher, Fritz, and Quarantelli (1956), Engel (1962), Belson (1967), and Cannell, Lawson, and Hausser (1975) indicate that the presence of a tape recorder does not affect survey data, although Belson finds a zero net effect produced by opposite small effects at upper and lower levels of socioeconomic status (SES). Our data from the study reported here agree with this finding; respondents who were not taped because of refusal or mechanical failure were no different from respondents who were taped, neither in levels of reporting nor in uneasiness about their effect. It is not surprising that third parties introduced by the interviewer do not affect responses; respondents are already answering in the presence of a stranger when they respond to the interviewer.

Response effects are more likely to occur when the third party knows the respondent and either does not know the true answer to some private or personal question or the true answer differs from what the third party has been led to believe. In the former situation, we would expect that respondents might refuse to answer the question or distort their answers to maintain privacy; in the latter situation, they might distort their answers to conform to the expectations of the third party. In other situations, the presence of a third party probably will seldom cause response effects. We know of only one published study that examined the effects of third parties on a topic where effects were likely.

Taietz (1962) compared the percentages of elderly Dutch respondents who favored extended family living situations when they were questioned alone, when their spouses were present, when their adult children were present, and when both spouses and children were present. Respondents were far more positive about sharing living quarters with their children when children were present than when spouses were present. Taietz's findings are reproduced in Table 50.

Other data are described by Maccoby and Maccoby (1954). They refer to a study of war veterans conducted by Stouffer and others (1949) in which "when the veteran's wife was present during the interview, he was more likely to complain about unfair treatment by the public than if she were not present, and he was less likely to express resentment toward civilians who asked him about his war experiences if others were present." We could not get the data for this finding. Stouffer and others (1949) do not mention the finding, and we cannot obtain the report in which the data might be described (Bureau of Agricultural Economics, 1945). However, third persons known to the respondent do seem to influence answers to some questions.

Design of the Study

These results are from the 1975 U.S. national sample survey of 1,172 adults described in Chapter Two. Interviewers were instructed to try to get all third parties out of the room before interviewing. If they could not persuade the third parties to leave, they

**Table 50. Percentage of Respondents Favoring an Extended Family
When Third Party Present**

Statement	None	Spouse	Spouse and Children	Children
Old People Are Happiest When They Live in the Same House with Their Children (Agree)	79	55	80	88
	(34)	(33)	(50)	(91)
It Is Better for a Young Married Couple to Have Their Own Home Than to Live in the Same House with Their Parents (Disagree)	12	3	12	21
	(32)	(34)	(41)	(75)
To Live with One's Children Is Very Desirable (Agree)	52	24	36	58
	(37)	(37)	(61)	(91)
If Had Choice, Would Live with Children (Agree)	58	22	60	78
	(36)	(36)	(62)	(94)

Source: Reprinted from Philip Taietz, "Conflicting Group Norms and the 'Third' Person
in the Interview," by permission of the *American Journal of Sociology* and the University of
Chicago Press. Copyright © 1962 by the University of Chicago.

were allowed to proceed with interviewing. The presence of third
parties was noted in "Interviewer Remarks," which the interviewers
completed as soon as possible after finishing interviews. Interviewers answered a question series that read:

> Was anyone else present during any part of the interview?
> Yes...(ANSWER A & B) 1
> No 2
> (If "Yes")
> A. Who was it?
> Spouse 1
> Child 2
> Parent 3
> Sibling 4
> Other (SPECIFY)_____ 5
>
> B. During which parts of the interview was someone else
>   present? (SPECIFY WHO IN WHICH PARTS:)

Three categories were broken out of the "other" group—adult friends, more than one child, and spouse and other. Unfortunately, we did not differentiate between spouse and other adult and spouse and child. Nonspecified relatives (cousins, uncles, and so forth) were almost never present.

How Often Are Third Parties Present?

The frequencies with which third parties were present during questioning ranged from 25.6 percent of the time for questions early in the interview to 19.0 percent for questions late in the interview. In 18.7 percent of the cases, the third party was present for the entire interview. This suggests that only a few third parties enter after the interview has begun. Most third parties are present from the start, and a fair number of them leave before the end.

Spouses and children were confirmed as the most common third parties. Spouses were present by themselves for 6.8 percent to 8.8 percent of the time and with someone else for an additional 1.5 percent to 2.0 percent of the time. One child was present 4.8 percent to 6.5 percent of the time; more than one child was present 1.5 percent to 2.0 percent of the time; and at least one child was present in probably 1.0 percent of the spouse-plus-other cases.

We certainly would not have expected third parties to be present in one fourth of the interviews, although this figure agrees with informal estimates interviewers have provided. The figure is surprisingly high, especially when one considers that these were top-rated interviewers who had been trained to get third parties out, if possible.

Some of the demographic characteristics of respondents for whom third parties were present are interesting. About 75 percent of the respondents for whom a spouse alone was present are men. This figure compares with 60 percent males when spouse and other were present and with 46 percent males in the overall sample. One can explain the differences by noting that men are much more likely to be interviewed when both partners are at home, but this situation provides the basis for the stereotype of the wife listening to the interview with her husband. About 80 percent of the respondents for whom one child was present and about 90 percent of the respondents for whom more than one child was present are women, supporting the stereotype of the mother supervising children. All third-party-present groups are younger than the norm except the spouse-present respondents. Somewhat surprisingly, respondents for whom third parties were present do not appear to be much lower in SES than respondents interviewed alone.

How Do Third Parties Affect Response?

Tables 51, 52, 53, and 54 present analyses of the effects of third parties on the data. These tables show that third-party effects are not a widespread phenomenon and give lukewarm support to the position that particular third parties affect particular items. Three dependent variables are considered—respondent's perceptions of how uneasy topics would make most people, item refusal rates, and actual reporting.

Table 51 shows the impact of third parties on the number of respondents who say that questions about a topic would make most people very uneasy. As discussed in Chapter Five, asking respondents how uneasy most people would feel produces a better measure of uneasiness than a direct question, and respondents who answer "very uneasy" have particularly large response effects. As a result, we want to minimize the number of people answering "very uneasy," both to avoid making the survey a disagreeable experience and to minimize response effects.

The numbers in Table 51 are the ratios of actual to expected numbers of respondents saying "very uneasy." To form the expectations, we began with the proportions of respondents for whom no third party was present who answered "very uneasy." These proportions were adjusted to control for differences in age and education levels between respondents for whom various types of third parties were present and respondents for whom third parties were not present. Age and education were controlled, because respondents for whom third parties were present generally were somewhat younger and better educated, and because previous analyses had shown age and education to be the only background variables that affected uneasiness. The adjusted figures were estimated proportions of respondents in each group who would have said "very uneasy" if the third parties had no effect. These estimates were divided into the actual numbers encountered to form Table 51. For example, we would have expected 55.68 percent of the

Table 51. Ratios of Actual to Expected Percentages of Very Uneasy Respondents When Third Party Present

	Type of Third Party															
	Any				Spouse				Friend				One Child			
Topic	Expected	Actual	Ratio		Expected	Actual	Ratio		Expected	Actual	Ratio		Expected	Actual	Ratio	
Gambling	9.7	10.2	1.05	(264)	13.5	8.4	.63	(83)	8.6	9.1	1.06	(43)	7.5	14.3	1.92	(76)
Drinking Beer, Wine, or Liquor	9.1	11.6	1.27	(275)	11.5	10.1	.88	(89)	8.1	8.9	1.10	(44)	7.8	11.5	1.49	(77)
Getting Drunk	28.0	26.9	.96	(277)	32.5	28.9	.89	(90)	27.7	30.4	1.10	(45)	25.4	26.9	1.06	(77)
Using Marijuana	39.0	45.6	1.17	(267)	43.5	47.6	1.10	(84)	39.2	43.5	1.11	(45)	39.2	50.7	1.29	(69)
Using Stimulants or Depressants	32.1	30.8	.96	(258)	33.1	34.2	1.03	(85)	31.6	30.4	.96	(45)	31.8	30.0	.94	(69)
Petting or Kissing	19.1	21.0	1.10	(246)	20.3	22.1	1.09	(86)	20.2	12.2	.61	(48)	18.3	25.4	1.38	(62)
Sexual Intercourse	40.9	40.5	.99	(245)	41.0	40.7	.99	(86)	41.8	35.4	.85	(47)	40.4	50.8	1.26	(62)
Masturbation	56.1	56.2	1.00	(241)	55.9	54.2	.97	(83)	55.7	46.8	.82	(47)	57.4	71.4	1.28	(62)
Income	11.2	13.7	1.22	(254)	15.3	17.4	1.14	(82)	11.1	14.3	1.28	(48)	9.3	6.7	.72	(59)

respondents who had one child present to say that answering questions about masturbation would make most people very uneasy; 71.43 percent of these respondents gave that answer. The ratio of 71.43 to 55.68, or 1.28, appears in the appropriate cell of Table 51.

We did not have any firm expectations about the impact of third parties on respondent uneasiness. We thought that respondents might be more uneasy about discussing threatening topics, particularly sex, in front of children. Since the presence of more than one child suggests that the children's attention will be diverted by play, one child was expected to cause more uneasiness than more than one child. We did not expect spouses to cause greater uneasiness, because, except in rare cases, the spouses would already know the answers. Respondents were expected to feel more uneasy about answering the income question, and possibly other threatening items, when persons outside the family were present. Other topics and types of third parties were excluded from consideration, because not enough respondents rated the topic as making people very uneasy, or because not enough respondents fell into the group.

Table 51 generally confirms our expectations. Spouses had no impact on uneasiness. Friends also had no impact, but the difference in uneasiness about reporting income was in the expected direction. One child did have an impact—more respondents than expected said "very uneasy" for seven of the nine items, and five of these differences were significant using a one-tailed test (masturbation was significant at .01; intercourse, gambling, and marijuana at .05; and petting or kissing at .10). The data where more than one child was present were not merged with the one-child data because they were dissimilar, although they did not exhibit any reliable pattern.

Table 52 presents the effect of third parties on item refusals. The expected refusal rates were calculated in a manner similar to that used for the expected uneasiness rates in Table 51. Only the three sexual-behavior items and the income item were used, because other items had too few refusals to support analysis. Since "don't know" responses may often be a polite way of refusing to report income, both refusals and "don't knows" are shown for the income question.

We expected all types of third parties to stimulate more refusals on all four items, with especially large effects on the sex

Table 52. Ratios of Actual to Expected Percentages of Item Refusals When Third Party Present

		Type of Third Party										
	Any			Spouse			Friend			One Child		
Topic	Expected	Actual	Ratio	Expected	Actual	Ratio	Expected	Actual	Ratio	Expected	Actual	Ratio
Petting or Kissing Past Month	2.7	6.7	2.48 (253)	2.9	8.8	3.03 (91)	2.7	6.3	2.33 (48)	2.5	3.2	1.28 (62)
Intercourse Past Month	5.1	9.9	1.94 (253)	4.9	13.2	2.69 (91)	5.0	8.3	1.67 (48)	5.1	6.5	1.27 (62)
Masturbation Past Month	5.6	11.1	1.98 (253)	5.9	17.6	2.98 (91)	5.4	8.3	1.54 (48)	5.3	4.8	.91 (62)
Income	4.4	6.1	1.39 (262)	4.6	8.2	1.78 (98)	4.3	4.2	.98 (48)	4.0	1.7	.43 (59)
Income, "Don't Knows" Plus Refusals	10.6	11.1	1.05 (262)	10.9	11.2	1.03 (98)	10.5	12.5	1.19 (48)	10.3	5.1	.50 (59)

items when a child was present and the income item when a friend was present. Very large increases did appear, but not where we had expected them. Increases in refusals were particularly sharp for the sex items when the spouse or a friend was present.

The last group of analyses considered the effects of third parties on reporting, or the direct relationship between third parties and response effects. Tables 53 and 54 show the results. These analyses are presented last, because the issue of nonrandom samples is most troublesome for them. More variables seem to affect the actual and reported levels of attitudes and behaviors than affect uneasiness about questions or refusals to answer. To minimize this concern, the expectations used in forming Tables 53 and 54 were calculated with controls for sex, race, South versus non-South location, and SMSA versus non-SMSA location, as well as age and education groups. Unfortunately, number of children was not available as a control.

Table 53 covers the key behavioral items associated with the uneasiness results in Table 51, plus two questions that were asked about the behavior of the respondent's three closest friends. Since differing norms or expectations between the respondent and the third party are important to third-party effects, we did not expect spouses to cause response effects for these items. Spouses should know the correct levels of behaviors for their partners. Terman (1938), Kinsey and others (1948, 1953), and Clark and Wallin (1964) have indicated that 33 percent to 77 percent of pairs of husbands and wives disagree in reporting how often they have sex, but most of these disagreements amount to only one incident per month. Clark and Wallin show that the major disagreements occur when the wife is sated and overreports. Husbands seem to report accurately even in these cases, and most of our respondents for whom a spouse was present are men.

Also, the knowledge that the presence of a friend did not affect reported uneasiness led us to expect no effects on reported behavior. We did expect that respondents would hesitate to report that their friends became intoxicated or used marijuana when a friend was present, and we expected the presence of a child to cause underreporting. However, no stable, predictable effects appear in Table 53 for any type of third party. This result is surprising and encouraging.

Table 53. Ratios of Actual to Expected Percentages of Respondents Reporting Threatening Behaviors When Third Party Present

| | Type of Third Party | | | | | | | | | | | |
| | Any | | | Spouse | | | Friend | | | One Child | | |
Topic	Expected	Actual	Ratio	Expected	Actual	Ratio	Expected	Actual	Ratio	Expected	Actual	Ratio
Gambling Scale[a]	1.02	1.00	.98 (257)	1.22	.77	.63 (85)	.92	1.37	1.48 (41)	.92	1.03	1.12 (73)
Ever Drink Beer	80.3	81.9	1.02 (265)	84.3	87.8	1.04 (90)	79.2	83.3	1.05 (42)	75.2	77.8	1.03 (72)
Ever Drink Wine	81.2	81.4	1.00 (264)	83.2	84.4	1.01 (90)	81.6	83.3	1.02 (42)	78.2	81.7	1.04 (71)
Ever Drink Liquor	83.1	86.0	1.03 (265)	86.0	92.2	1.07 (90)	81.1	92.9	1.15 (42)	80.0	76.4	.96 (72)
Drunk Past Year	31.8	32.8	1.03 (262)	31.5	27.0	.86 (89)	30.9	31.0	1.00 (42)	30.9	27.8	.90 (72)
Three Best Friends Drunk Past Year[b]	1.07	1.08	1.01 (244)	1.07	.84	.78 (80)	1.06	1.40	1.32 (38)	1.04	.90	.87 (68)
Ever Smoke Marijuana	23.7	21.2	.89 (250)	20.6	13.6	.66 (88)	26.5	37.2	1.40 (43)	24.6	17.2	.70 (64)
Three Best Friends Smoked Marijuana[b]	.66	.59	.90 (234)	.57	.42	.73 (84)	.69	1.07	1.55 (41)	.75	.38	.50 (58)
Ever Use Stimulants	12.2	11.6	.95 (250)	11.2	5.7	.51 (88)	14.6	18.6	1.27 (43)	12.3	14.1	1.15 (64)
Ever Use Depressants	9.8	10.0	1.02 (250)	9.0	6.8	.76 (88)	10.4	18.6	1.79 (43)	10.4	7.8	.75 (64)
Petting or Kissing Past Month	79.3	79.8	1.01 (223)	75.6	80.0	1.06 (80)	74.8	74.4	.99 (43)	82.4	80.4	.98 (56)
Intercourse Past Month	71.0	73.6	1.04 (216)	68.9	71.4	1.04 (77)	71.2	69.0	.97 (42)	74.1	77.8	1.05 (54)
Masturbation Past Month	9.5	10.8	1.14 (213)	10.5	9.6	.91 (73)	9.0	19.5	2.17 (41)	9.0	5.5	.61 (55)
Income	$13,566	$12,175	.90 (235)	$13,339	$10,627	.80 (92)	$13,782	$12,471	.90 (42)	$13,366	$13,392	1.00 (53)

[a] Number reported out of six gambling activities.

Table 54. Ratios of Actual to Expected Reporting of Satisfaction When Third Party Present

	Type of Third Party											
	Any			Spouse			Friend			One Child		
Topic	Expected	Actual	Ratio	Expected	Actual	Ratio	Expected	Actual	Ratio	Expected	Actual	Ratio
Satisfaction with Leisure Activities	3.67	3.81	1.04 (299)	3.70	4.00	1.08 (102)	3.66	3.67	1.00 (58)	3.65	3.84	1.05 (76)
Satisfaction with House or Apartment	3.85	3.86	.99 (300)	3.97	3.88	.98 (104)	3.79	3.63	.96 (57)	3.83	3.66	.95 (76)
Satisfaction with Neighborhood	3.67	3.73	1.02 (301)	3.81	3.73	.98 (104)	3.58	3.71	1.04 (58)	3.61	3.70	1.02 (76)
Satisfaction with Financial Situation	3.00	2.99	1.00 (301)	3.16	3.16	1.00 (104)	2.87	2.57	.89 (58)	2.97	3.12	1.05 (76)
Satisfaction with Health	3.08	3.05	.99 (300)	2.98	2.98	1.00 (104)	3.12	3.02	.97 (57)	3.13	3.16	1.01 (76)
Satisfaction with Job	3.75	3.84	1.02 (149)	3.83	3.89	1.02 (56)	3.72	3.59	.97 (32)	3.72	4.16	1.12 (31)
Satisfaction with Marriage	4.33	4.44	1.03 (235)	4.40	4.57	1.04 (100)	4.29	4.28	1.00 (29)	4.30	4.40	1.02 (63)
Satisfaction with Life as a Whole	3.80	3.89	1.02 (300)	3.84	3.98	1.04 (103)	3.77	3.86	1.02 (58)	3.79	3.95	1.04 (76)

Scale: 1 = not at all satisfied, 5 = completely satisfied.

Attitudinal items generally are more susceptible to response effects than behavioral items, so we also examined the impacts of third parties on reports of satisfaction. Table 54 gives the results of these analyses. We expected respondents to report higher levels of satisfaction for all items and all types of third parties. Presence of the spouse was expected to have an especially large impact on reported marital satisfaction. Once again, we were encouraged by a finding of no effects.

Conclusions

The data presented in this chapter suggest that survey data generally are immune to the presence of third parties while information is gathered. The presence of one child seems to make respondents more uneasy about discussing threatening behaviors, and adult third parties seem to stimulate a higher item-refusal rate. However, actual reporting does not seem to be affected by the presence of third parties.

Third parties are an inescapable fact in face-to-face household surveys. Someone other than the interviewer and respondent was present in one fourth of the interviews conducted for this study, despite the use of top-rated interviewers and training instructions to avoid interviewing in the presence of third parties if possible. Researchers who are worried about respondent uneasiness and item-refusal rates, or who see problems in our reporting data and the Taietz data, have one more reason to consider switching to telephone interviewing. Third parties usually can hear only the answers (or the questions) in telephone interviews.

Of course, third-party effects not considered by these data may exist. We do not know whether the presence of third parties increases respondents' resistance to be interviewed and thus case refusals. Also, the most powerful response effects in these data clearly occurred when a young adult respondent was interviewed with a parent present. There were not enough cases in this group to justify presenting the data, but researchers who are working with large samples of young respondents may find interesting results in analyzing the impact of parental presence. It may be that intergenerational third-party effects are far larger than intragenerational effects. Certainly, there is room for more research into the effects of third parties on survey data.

Chapter Nine

Asking Respondents About Friends' Behavior

Faced with the substantial response effects to threatening questions discussed earlier, are there any other possible data sources? Monroe Sirken (Office of Substance Abuse Services, 1975) has suggested using questions about friends' behavior as another approach to improving data on threatening topics. Questions about friends' behavior can replace or supplement the usual questions about respondents' behavior in estimating total levels of behavior. These questions are not, however, surrogates for the respondent's

Note: Adapted from Seymour Sudman, Edward Blair, Norman M. Bradburn, and Carol Stocking, "Estimates of Threatening Behavior Based on Reports of Friends," *Public Opinion Quarterly,* Summer 1977, *41,* 261–264.

own behavior and cannot be cross-classified by respondent characteristics. The following question illustrates this approach: "Think
of your three closest friends. (Don't mention their names.) As far
as you know, how many of them have ever smoked marijuana?"

Questions about friends' behavior may have three advantages over standard questions about respondent's behavior for estimating total levels of behavior. First, since friends' names are never
obtained, the data for friends are completely anonymous. This
anonymity prevents any possible legal reprisal and reduces concern about invasion of privacy. Second, underreporting may be
reduced, so that the reported level is nearer to actual behavior.
Finally, the sampling error of estimates based on clusters of three
friends will almost always be smaller than the sampling error of
estimates based on individual data.

Improvement in Reporting

The national study discussed in Chapter Two collected respondent and friends' data for three questions, one dealing with
intoxication in the past year and two dealing with marijuana use
in the past year or ever.

Table 55 compares respondents' reports about themselves
and about their three closest friends. For the questions about being
intoxicated and about smoking marijuana in the past year, reported
behavior for the three closest friends is higher than for self. However, reported behavior for self is slightly higher than reported
behavior for friends on the question about having ever smoked
marijuana.

The results on marijuana smoking in the past year are virtually identical to the results obtained by Sirken in Michigan, although
he asked about the percentage of closest friends without specifying
the number of friends. Sirken's estimate of the percentage of persons smoking marijuana in the past year based on self-reports was
11.3 percent, compared with the 11.6 percent estimate obtained in
this study. The Michigan estimate based on closest friends was 16.2
percent, compared with this estimate of 15.5 percent.

These results suggest that reports about closest friends yield
better data than self-reports for threatening behavior in the past
year, but that estimates based on reports of closest friends ever

Table 55. Reported Behavior for Self and Three Closest Friends by Perceived Threat of Questions

	Percentage			
	(I) Self	(II) Three Closest Friends	(III) Ratio (II)/(I)	N
Ever Intoxicated Past Year	31.4	34.5	1.10	1,054
Respondent Very Uneasy	24.2	25.9	1.07	303
Moderately Uneasy	36.5	39.5	1.08	223
Slightly Uneasy	38.0	41.7	1.10	315
Not at All Uneasy	27.0	30.8	1.14	213
Ever Smoked Marijuana	21.6	19.7	.91	1,088
Respondent Very Uneasy	18.2	18.7	1.03	449
Moderately Uneasy	32.3	27.8	.86	210
Slightly Uneasy	26.4	20.9	.79	214
Not at All Uneasy	14.2	12.6	.89	215
Smoked Marijuana Past Year	11.6	15.5	1.34	1,091
Respondent Very Uneasy	10.9	14.9	1.37	456
Moderately Uneasy	16.1	22.4	1.39	205
Slightly Uneasy	15.4	16.3	1.06	215
Not at All Uneasy	4.9	9.4	1.92	215

engaging in an activity are less useful. An obvious reason is that many friendships are not of lifelong duration.

It might be expected that differences between reports about friends' behavior and self-reports would vary by level of respondent uneasiness, but this is not the case, as seen in Table 55. Additional analyses comparing self-reported behavior and behavior of friends also show no effect by level of uneasiness.

Sampling Errors of Estimates Based on Clusters of Three Closest Friends

The sampling variance of estimates based on individuals cannot be smaller than the sampling variance of estimates based on clusters of their three closest friends. The clusters of three friends provide an equivalent sample size between one and three times the individual sample size. The correlation *rho* among the reported behavior of friends will determine the reduction in sampling variance of estimates.

For the dichotomous questions reported in Table 55, the rho's are substantial, averaging about .62 for each of the three items. This is because the largest number of respondents reported that none of their three closest friends engaged in the activity, and the second largest group reported that all three closest friends engaged in the activity. Thus, for those three items, the sampling variance for estimates about three closest friends is about .75 that of estimates for individuals (see Sudman, 1976, 73–78).

Of course, sampling variance is only one part of total response error. For private activities such as sexual behavior, media use, and many purchase variables, estimates about friends would be guesses subject to a high degree of unreliability. This increase in response unreliability would swamp the reduction in sampling variance and lead to greater total error. Estimates based on friends would be inappropriate for these private activities.

Conclusions

Our results indicate that asking about the respondent's three closest friends instead of the respondent produces some increase in reporting for threatening questions about behavior in the past year. This increase is general and is not restricted to respondents who are very uneasy about the question. In addition, the sampling variances of estimates based on friends are reduced even when the correlation of behavior among friends is sizable. Although the data are limited, the results are encouraging enough to make further testing of this procedure desirable.

The validity of this procedure rests on several assumptions. The first is that individuals do in fact know about their friends' behavior. For some types of sensitive behavior this assumption seems plausible, for others not. For example, respondents should know whether or not their friends drink alcoholic beverages, but they might be poorer reporters about the frequency or quantity of their friends' drinking. They might be much less likely to know whether or not their friends cheat on their income tax returns.

To use this method well, we need to know more about the kinds of sensitive behaviors that people confide to their friends but will not tell strangers. We particularly need to know how these behaviors differ from those they are more willing to tell strangers in a confidential interview than they are willing to tell their friends.

In general, we suspect that the technique is more adapted to making estimates about whether something has ever happened or happens regularly (for example, have your friends ever smoked marijuana, or do they get drunk at least once a month?) rather than to making estimates about quantity or frequency of behavior (how often do your friends smoke marijuana, or how much liquor did they drink in the past week?).

A second assumption is that reporting for friends will be less subject to distortion than reporting about one's self because of the anonymity of the reports. Complete anonymity can be guaranteed by this method because it is not necessary to name the friends. Indeed, it is just those cases in which the investigator suspects there will be great reluctance to report about one's self—for example, about criminal or socially disapproved behavior—that the method recommends itself. One assumes that the greater accuracy of reporting that comes from removing the threat of self-incrimination more than makes up for any lack of knowledge the respondents might have about their friends' behavior.

Note that this method is not the same as using projective questions. Projective questions are those about other people's opinions or behavior that are assumed to be projections of the respondents' own feelings or behavior. We might consider the types of questions we asked about whether most people would feel uneasy in talking about a particular topic (as discussed in Chapter Five) as projective questions because we asked about a vaguely defined group, that is, "most people," rather than about specific individuals, "your three best friends." With projective situations the referent is deliberately vague to encourage respondents to add their own feelings and behavior to the reports. But in the "three best friends" question, we are specifically interested in veridical reports about specific, though unnamed, individuals and not about the respondents. In projective questions, we consider that the responses say something about their own beliefs or opinions and use the information in further cross tabulations. But with the "three best friends" question we treat the data as reports about three separate individuals who might have been interviewed. We consider these data to be real reports of behavior by individuals and use them to make estimates for a population, using the appropriate sampling variance estimates.

Chapter Ten

Problems in Using Imprecise Quantifying Words

In surveys, we frequently ask respondents to make judgments about "how much," "how often," "how strongly," and the like. Such judgments are most often made in terms of sets of ordered categories, such as "very often, pretty often, not too often"; "often, sometimes, never"; "too little, about right, too much"; and "below average, average, above average." We assume that the quantifiers are ordered in their intensity, but we know little about the characteristics of such adverbs. For example, do these imprecise quantifiers actually have some common meaning that is more pre-

Note: Adapted from Norman M. Bradburn and Carrie Miles, "Vague Quantifiers," *Public Opinion Quarterly,* forthcoming.

cise than is apparent on the surface? Do they mean the same thing to each respondent, or are variations in meaning patterned in some discoverable way? Does the meaning depend not only on the quantifier itself but also on the context in which it is used—for example, on the word it modifies or on the other quantifiers used in the set? Previous research gives us some clues to the types of problems that are apt to arise, although not full understanding.

An early study on quantifying meaning (Mosier, 1941) noted that the meaning of a word varied for each individual and in each context in which the word was used. Mosier postulated that word meaning had two components—one constant, anchoring meaning in the vicinity of a particular point on a continuum; and one variable, representing fluctuations in meaning due to the individual usage of the speaker and the context. If measured over a large group of speakers, the mean of the distribution represents the constant, individual responses to meaning arranged in a normal distribution around that point. Data from Mosier's study and that of Jones and Thurstone (1955) support this interpretation.

Mosier's 1941 study also included a set of words modified by adverbial intensifiers—for example, "very, quite, completely, extremely." These intensifiers seem to shift the meaning of the base word toward the extremes of the continuum.

Simpson (1944) attempted to quantify meaning along slightly different lines. Dealing with frequency words, Simpson asked his subjects to indicate the proportion of times out of 100 the stimulus word represented. Subjects were asked, for example, to what proportion "sometimes" referred. Hakel (1968) repeated the study with some variation and obtained results that correlated highly with Simpson's. Hakel noted that "variability is rampant. One man's 'rarely' is another man's 'hardly ever.'" But he found considerable stability in overall distributions. Wide individual variability may be compatible with stable group variation.

Cliff (1959) studied the effect of adding words similar to Mosier's intensifiers that act like multipliers. These words, such as "quite, very, unusually," have no value of their own but act to stretch the meaning of the words they modify. Cliff's subjects rated sets of modified evaluative adjectives on an unfavorable-neutral-favorable continuum. The results supported Cliff's hypothesis that the "common adverbs of degree multiply the intensity of the adjectives they modify" (p. 43). For example, he found that "very" multiplied the unfavorable-favorable scale value of an adjective or adverb it modified by about 1.317; "slightly" modified the adjective by about 0.55. If these results have applicability to the responses of subjects in survey conditions, then one might expect respondents to consider "very often" to be 1.317 times as frequent as "often." If one could confirm such values, one might use information about the scale intervals to construct continuous rather than merely ordered scales, assuming that individual variation is not too great.

The view that meaning is precise and may be specified as a point on a continuum or intersection of continua is explicit in these studies. That view has been challenged by Parducci (1968), Chase (1969), and Pepper and Prytulak (1974), who point out that the context within which words appear is important in establishing their meaning. Chase devised two scales using Hakel's terms, one of which was composed of low-frequency terms ("seldom, not often, once in a while, occasionally, generally") and the other of higher-frequency terms ("occasionally, now and then, about as often as not, usually, very often"). Thirty-four students rated their use of ten different study methods using each of these scales. Chase hypothesized that if people actually responded to the meaning of the words, the responses to the high-frequency scale would be quite different from the responses to the low-frequency scale. In fact, Chase found that the differences between the two scales were small. He concluded that "respondents get a good deal of meaning from scale adjectives because of the adjectives' relative position in a group of response categories, rather than in terms of a 'standard' definition of a given word out of context of other category levels" (p. 1043).

In the Pepper and Prytulak (1974) study, subjects provided numerical definitions of terms used in contexts that varied in frequency. In a low-frequency context, one of five terms—"very often, frequently, sometimes, seldom, almost never"—was embedded in the following paragraph:

> The *Stanford Daily* reported that, during 1951, California (frequency term) had sizable earthquakes. One would estimate that, during 1951, there were sizable earthquakes on about _____ days out of every 100.

Since earthquakes (and airplane crashes, the other low-frequency event) are not common occurrences, these were held to be low-frequency events. High-frequency events, such as the occurrence of shooting in Hollywood westerns, and moderate-frequency events, such as a student's missing breakfast, were also included. The results of this study showed that subjects did indeed perceive the frequencies of these events as the experimenters had expected. Further, they indicated that the numerical estimate for each term increased as the expected frequency for each term increased. Thus, the mean response for "sometimes" in the shooting in Hollywood westerns context is higher than the mean response for "very often" in the context of earthquakes. In short, "often" for an improbable event is less than "often" for a highly probable event. A related study by Bass, Cascio, and O'Connor (1974), however, failed to find differences in the values assigned to quantifiers when the context was varied according to the importance of the topic about which opinions were solicited. A critical difference here may have been between quantifiers applied to events or behavior and quantifiers applied to attitudes or beliefs.

Another approach to the study of meaning looks at individual differences rather than contextual differences. Goocher (1965), drawing on Helson's (1964) adaptation-level theory, predicted a negative relationship between a favorable attitude toward or participation in an activity and the frequency term selected to describe the median frequency of the occurrence of that event. Data from this study suggest that subjects who engage less in an activity or have a less-favorable attitude toward it are more likely than involved or favorable subjects to describe the actual median frequency of the occurrence of the event as "often" or "frequently." This difference appears to result from differences in the perceived median for the activity. Those who do not engage in the activity or do so very infrequently appear to believe that the median frequency is lower than it actually is; thus they describe the actual median with higher-level quantifiers. People who are actively engaged in the activity or are favorable to it perceive the median as higher than it actually is and thus use lower-level quantifiers. For example, respondents who dislike eating alone describe eating alone three times per week with adverbs that denote greater frequency than subjects who like eating alone, and respondents who "rarely" eat alone describe three times per week using adverbs that denote greater frequency than those who "often" eat alone.

Design of the Study

Data to begin an exploration of vague quantifiers in surveys come from the experimental survey described in Chapter Two. In this survey, we asked respondents about a series of feeling states they might have experienced during the recent past. For example, we asked how often during the past few weeks respondents had felt particularly excited or interested in something and how often they had felt bored. Respondents were asked to answer in terms of a four-point scale that was labeled "never, not too often, pretty often, or very often." At the conclusion of the set of ten questions, five reflecting positive states and five reflecting negative states, we asked respondents about the meaning of the response category they had chosen for the positive and negative items that were least often reported as never having been experienced. For example, we asked those who reported that they had felt excited or interested in something during the past few weeks "very often" exactly how many times a day or week they meant when they said "very often"; we asked the same individuals how often they meant by the response category they had used for the item about feeling bored. Thus, each individual was asked about one response category for one positive and one negative item. It would have been nice to have estimates for each degree of "often" from each respondent, but we felt that this would be too much to ask of the respondents in this survey.

In general, interviewers reported that giving a more precise meaning to degrees of "often" was difficult for respondents, and that they were reluctant to give responses. However, only 5 to 6 percent finally said they did not know or otherwise refused to give a response.

Results

The mean frequencies and the standard deviations for each of the response categories are given in Table 56. Respondents reported in their own terms. The responses were then converted

Table 56. Means and Standard Deviations of Responses to "How Often Is _____ Often?" (Times per Month)

	Response Categories	Excited	Bored
	Not Too Often	6.65	4.15
		(327)	(552)
Means	Pretty Often	12.95	13.72
		(495)	(127)
	Very Often	17.73	17.39
		(247)	(99)
	Not Too Often	8.57	5.71
Standard Deviations	Pretty Often	12.11	10.64
	Very Often	15.00	13.09

into the number of times per month (taking a month as equal to four weeks, if the responses were given in terms of times per week, and twenty-eight days, if responses were given in terms of times per day). Respondents who reported that they "never" felt excited or bored are, of course, omitted from this table.

If we take these estimates of frequency as rough estimates of the distance between the response categories or the degree to which the modifying terms change the meaning of "often," we see that, although the categories are ordered as we would suppose, the distance between the categories is not the same. It is further from "not too often" to "pretty often" than it is from "pretty often" to "very often." If we think of "times per month" as our metric for excited or interested in something, the distance between "not too often" and "pretty often" is 6.30 times per month, while the distance between "pretty often" and "very often" is only 4.78 times per month. For bored, it is 9.57 times per month between "not too often" and "pretty often," while "very often" is only 3.67 times per month greater than "pretty often."

Perhaps a better way of looking at these data is to consider the category "pretty often" as equivalent to "often" unmodified. (There is evidence from Hakel, 1968, that this assumption is warranted.) Then we might think of the modifier "not too" as multiplying the meaning of "often" by .51 for excited and .30 for bored, and the effect of the modifier "very" is to multiply the meaning of "often" by 1.37 for excited and 1.27 for bored. Or, to put it in round numbers, "not too often" is about 50 to 70 percent less than "often," and "very often" is about 30 percent more. The value of about 1.3 for "very" is similar to that obtained by Cliff (1959).

Note also that there is some support for the hypothesis that the meaning of quantifiers may change in relation to the overall frequency of the event. For the sample as a whole, being excited or interested in something is more frequent than is being bored. Ninety-eight percent of the sample reported feeling excited or interested in something at least once during the past few weeks, while only 70 percent reported feeling bored at least once. When we look at the meaning assigned to the phrase "not too often," we see that it is 2.5 times per month less for bored than for excited or interested. For the other two categories, however, there is very little difference between the frequency estimates given for the two feeling states. Pepper and Prytulak (1974) found that the meaning of specific frequency terms was lower for rare events than for more common events. Since we are not dealing with events whose occurrence is as discrepant as Pepper and Prytulak's (earthquakes and shooting in westerns), we should not expect to find differences as substantial as they did.

Another way of exploring the relationship between the frequency of the occurrence of events and the meaning given to vague quantifiers is to look at the relationship between scores on two scales, one made up of responses to all the items related to positive feelings and one made up of responses to all the items related to negative feelings. This type of scale, which was developed in other contexts (see Bradburn, 1969), is constructed by giving equal weights to each of the different response categories—for example, zero for "never" through a score of three for "very often"—and summing across the five positive items or five negative items. Thus, for each scale, the scores could range from zero to fifteen. If there is a relationship between the frequency of occurrence of a feeling state and the meaning assigned to the quantifiers, we would expect that those who are high on the positive or negative affect scale would report, for example, that "very often" means more times per month than would those who are low on the positive or negative affect scale.

In general, the data shown in Table 57 support this hypothesis, although the differences in assigned frequencies are not large

Table 57. (A) Mean Times per Month Excited by Positive Affect and (B) Mean Times per Month Bored by Negative Affect

(A)

Response Category	Positive Affect					
	Low (0–8)		Medium (9–10)		High (11–15)	
	$\overline{x}$	S.D.	$\overline{x}$	S.D.	$\overline{x}$	S.D.
Not Too Often	6.7 (266)	8.9	7.4 (43)	7.3	—	—
Pretty Often	11.0 (142)	9.8	12.9 (251)	9.7	15.7 (100)	18.6
Very Often	[12.3] (19)	12.2	14.9 (60)	16.3	19.3 (164)	15.2

(B)

Response Category	Negative Affect					
	Low (0–4)		Medium (5–6)		High (7–15)	
	$\overline{x}$	S.D.	$\overline{x}$	S.D.	$\overline{x}$	S.D.
Not Too Often	3.6 (168)	3.5	4.3 (292)	6.9	4.8 (88)	4.6
Pretty Often	—	—	8.9 (32)	8.7	15.3 (91)	10.8
Very Often	—	—	—	—	17.3 (92)	13.3

for the category "not too often." For the meaning of "very often," those who score high on positive affect (scores from 11 to 15) report a mean frequency of 19.3 times per month, as compared with a mean frequency of 12.3 times per month by those who score low on positive affect (scores from 0 to 8). Not only are those high on the positive affect scale more likely to have reported that they felt excited or interested in something "very often," but they also appear to mean more times per month by that response category than those lower on the scale. Similar differences are found for the frequencies assigned to the categories "pretty often" and "very often" among those who differ in scores on the negative affect scale. Note, however, that for all these estimates, the standard deviations are quite large.

Having demonstrated some of the differences in the values

assigned to the response categories that we typically treat as equal-interval categories, how might we use this information in our analysis? One way might be to use the empirical estimates of frequency to weight responses differentially instead of equally. Ideally, we would like each respondent to have given a separate estimate of the frequency he or she would assign to each response category for each item. Then we could weight by individual meaning. But here we do not have such complete individual estimates, so we can only use average values. Given the large standard deviations of these estimates, we should not be surprised if the use of average values does not alter the interpretations very much.

As an example of how such a procedure might go, let us look at the relationship between the positive and negative affect scales and overall ratings of life satisfaction and happiness under different weighting schemes for the various response categories. Table 58 presents data for the positive and negative affect scales constructed under different assumptions about the values to be as-

Table 58. Correlations and Regression Coefficients for Positive Affect, Negative Affect, and Life Satisfaction Using Different Values for "How Often"

(A) Correlations

Response Categories (Values of "Often")	Positive Affect/ Negative Affect	Positive Affect/ Life Satisfaction	Negative Affect/ Life Satisfaction
1. Valued Equally	−.079	.317	−.338
2. Valued by Frequency	−.265	.380	−.363
3. Valued by Ratios (Pretty Often = 1)	−.266	.381	−.363

(B) Regression Coefficients for Regression of Life Satisfaction on Positive and Negative Affect

		Betas (S.E.)	
Response Categories	R^2	Positive Affect	Negative Affect
1. Valued Equally	.199	.292 (.009)	−.315 (.009)
2. Valued by Frequency	.218	.306 (.002)	−.282 (.002)
3. Valued by Ratios (Pretty Often = 1)	.219	.307 (.024)	−.281 (.022)

signed to the frequency categories. The table gives the correlations and the results of a regression of the life-satisfaction ratings on positive and negative affect. In the first set of figures, the values of 0, 1, 2, and 3 were assigned to the response categories "never," "not too often," "pretty often," and "very often," respectively. The correlation between positive and negative affect is low and negative, and each scale correlates with overall ratings of life satisfaction to about the same degree, although, of course, in opposite directions. The R^2 is .199.

The second set of figures (reported in Table 58) shows the values derived from the respondents' mean reports about how often was meant by each of the response categories. The effect of using these values is to give greater weight to the top two response categories and to weight the response "not too often" less for negative affect items than for positive affect items. Using these values to construct the scales changes the correlation between the scales substantially (from $-.079$ to $-.265$) and raises slightly the respective correlations with the overall ratings of life satisfaction. The R^2 is also increased slightly, from .199 to .218, but there is very little change in the beta coefficients. We should note, however, that the beta coefficients have now changed around somewhat, so that the beta for positive affect is now slightly higher than the beta for negative affect, and the standard errors are slightly smaller.

In the third set of figures, the values derived from the respondents' mean reports of how often was meant by each of the response categories were also used to construct the scales, but in this transformation the ratios of the mean frequency estimates were used instead of the frequency means themselves. In this case, "pretty often" was taken as the standard and set to 1. "Not too often" thus became .50 for the positive feeling-state items and .31 for the negative feeling-state items; the value for "very often" became 1.37 for the positive items and 1.27 for the negative items. We see that using the ratios instead of the frequencies produces nearly identical correlations among the scales and virtually the same R^2 and beta weights for the variables. It does, however, have the effect of substantially increasing the standard errors of the betas. Other transformations, using ratios based on "not too often" as 1 or using the logarithms of the values, produce substantially the same pattern of correlations and the same R^2.

Conclusions

Using information from estimates of the "oftenness" of different degrees of "often" does improve the explanatory power of the affect items a little and is worthy of further exploration. Although use of the mean values does not improve things greatly, the variance in the values is very large, and it is likely that substitution of individual estimates, which were not available in this study, would improve things to a considerable extent.

If one needs to rely on individual estimates for the more exact meaning of vague quantifiers, why not just ask for exact estimates in the first place and avoid the problem? We do not typically do this because of the difficulty respondents have with the task. Although it is relatively easy for respondents to report how many times in the past week they have been to a movie or how many hours they watched television yesterday, they seem to have a great deal of difficulty in putting precise numbers on subjective states and on events of relatively low salience. It would thus place too great a burden on respondents to have to make precise estimates for each item in a typical survey questionnaire. It does seem possible, however, that respondents could be asked to make one overall numerical estimate for frequency terms within the context of an interview. Further exploration of the benefits of using one-time individual estimates in the interpretation of data will determine whether or not it is worth putting even this slightly increased burden on respondents.

Chapter Eleven

Conclusions and Implications for Survey Practice

In this book, we have presented the results of a series of empirical studies designed to investigate response effects related to threatening questions—that is, questions on topics about which many respondents are reluctant to talk fully and honestly. In this chapter, we shall pull together the rather disparate results of our studies with an eye to improving the practice of survey research. We hope that the results of our studies will enable survey practitioners to improve their questionnaire design and to be sensitive in their analyses to possible biasing factors in the data.

Before turning to a discussion of the different factors related to response effects, we should remind readers that we are concerned here with threatening questions, not all questions that one

163

might ask respondents. Threatening questions are, almost by definition, questions that are more susceptible than nonthreatening ones to response effects. Thus, researchers need to be particularly careful when designing research involving such questions.

But how does one tell what is a threatening question? There is, of course, no magical or easy answer to that question. We started out, as do most researchers, by using our own experience and intuition about the kinds of questions most respondents might find threatening. For the most part, we were gratified to find that the data confirmed our intuitions, although there were some surprises —just enough surprises to warn us that we should not rely entirely on our own experience but should check things out empirically wherever possible.

We went about determining whether or not questions were threatening in two ways. The most direct way was to determine the amount of underreporting or overreporting of behavior by checking respondents' reports with external records. This method is expensive and time-consuming, and it is not always possible since many threatening behaviors cannot be checked against records and since questions about attitudes, by definition, are not susceptible to external-validity checks. However, record checks have been done for a variety of topics, and each researcher does not have to start fresh to determine the relative magnitudes of underreporting or overreporting. Unfortunately, there is at present no single source or ready reference to which researchers can turn for this information. Significant amounts of data are scattered about in the literature and ought to be collected.

In one of our own studies, we obtained data for five behaviors, some of which we assumed (correctly, as it turned out) would be susceptible to overreporting and some to underreporting. In general, our expectations about the degree of threat of the questions were confirmed, but there were two surprises. We had expected that questions about bankruptcy would be more threatening (more highly underreported) than questions about arrests for drunken driving, but this turned out not to be the case, although both questions were more threatening than questions about voter registration or library card ownership, which we expected to be low-threat questions. The biggest surprise, however, was that the degree of response distortion for the question about voting in the primary election (which had occurred shortly before the interviewing period) was almost as high as that for reports of arrests for drunken driving, but of course in the opposite direction, and higher than that for reports of bankruptcy. We had selected the primary voting question as a low-threat question, because we thought that it was well known that voting turnouts in primaries are low (particularly in Chicago, from which the sample was drawn), and that no particular stigma was attached to not voting in primaries. However, many respondents claimed to have voted, even though the records did not show them as having done so. Apparently, voting is a more sensitive issue than we thought.

The second method used to determine the relative threat of questions was to ask respondents directly to rate question topics as to how uneasy they thought most people would be in talking about the particular topic. We also asked about the respondents' own reactions to the questions, had interviewers rate the degree of difficulty the topics caused in the interview, and recorded the number of item refusals and "don't knows" to particular items. In general, all these methods produced about the same rankings of topics in degree of threat, and the rankings were roughly in accord with expectations about which questions would be threatening. Questions about sports and leisure activities appear to be nonthreatening; questions about drinking, gambling, and income appear to be moderately threatening; and questions about illicit drug use and sex were rated as quite threatening. Since respondents' ratings of the degree of threat of the topics, as measured by their perception of how most people react to the question (but not how they themselves reacted to the question), were related to their own reports of engaging in the behavior, we believe that this method of determining the relative threat of questions can be quite useful.

Since threatening questions present particularly difficult measurement problems, we feel it is important that researchers pay particular attention to their research instruments, asking themselves whether any of their questions are apt to fall into the threatening category. If so, they should pay special attention to all factors that might reduce the validity of the responses. As a rule of thumb, we would suggest that researchers should be particularly alert to the threatening nature of questions when more than 20 percent of the respondents feel that most people would be made very uneasy by talking about the topic. When between 10 and 20 percent of the respondents feel that most people would be very uneasy about a topic, the researcher is probably in an area that will have some threat problems, at least for some subgroups of the population, and should be alert for possible response effects.

Once researchers have determined that they are dealing with threatening questions, what should they pay attention to? In line with our general model for studying response effects, we shall discuss the results of our studies under three headings—the research task, the interviewer, and the respondent.

The Research Task

One of the more frequently considered aspects of the research task is the selection of the appropriate method of asking questions in research interviews. Face-to-face interviews involving personal interaction between interviewers and respondents have been thought of as potentially more open to bias than other, more impersonal forms of asking questions, such as self-administered forms, not only because of the possible biases introduced by interviewer behavior, but simply because the personal contact engages general norms about self-presentation that are thought to cause the respondents to distort their answers in the direction of making a more favorable impression on the interviewer. Thus, it is widely expected that, for threatening questions in which self-presentation may be a larger factor than in nonthreatening questions, the face-to-face interview might produce the least-valid responses. One particularly ingenious technique for introducing the advantages of complete anonymity within the face-to-face interview is the random response technique, which allows the respondent to answer questions without the interviewer knowing what question is being answered. Such a technique, if valid, would allow researchers to use regular face-to-face interviewing for most questions and reserve an anonymous technique for the most threatening questions, which might be most affected by the method of administration.

In our study, there was no clear-cut advantage for any particular method of administration of the questionnaire. We compared face-to-face, telephone, self-administered, and random response techniques for questions of differing degrees of threat. The random response technique did show some promise in reducing underreporting for the two threatening items in which underreporting was a problem (bankruptcy and drunken driving), but it did not reduce overreporting for the item on voting in the primary election; in fact, the random response method produced the largest amount of overreporting for this item. The general conclusion we draw from our own study, as well as from the more general review of the literature (Sudman and Bradburn, 1974), is that no one method is clearly superior to all others. Different methods may be appropriate for specific studies. The selection of the method of administration will be properly influenced more by other considerations, such as cost, access to the desired sample, and ease of administration, than by the superiority of a particular method in terms of getting more valid data. The possible exception to this general rule is that the random response technique does appear to produce less underreporting for very threatening questions, although it did not eliminate underreporting altogether for our most threatening issue. In contrast, the random response technique puts some severe limitations on data analysis and is best for estimating a single parameter—for example, the proportion of respondents who have declared bankruptcy. It may be a useful technique, but it is not a panacea.

If the method of administration makes relatively little difference, the construction of questions makes a great deal of difference. Perhaps the most dramatic finding in our studies was the discovery that changes in the form of the questions—using a long introduction to the question topic as compared with asking short, terse questions; leaving the answer format open rather than giving the respondent a precoded set of alternatives from which to choose an answer; and, to a considerably lesser extent, letting the respondents pick their own words to talk about sensitive topics—can increase the amount of reporting of behavior two to three times over the amount reported using the standard form of the questions. The size of these response effects indicates strongly that two of these question forms—the long introductions and open-ended response format—should always be used in asking about sensitive behavior. The other experimental form—using a respondent-supplied familiar word or expression to talk about sensitive behavior—makes less difference, is somewhat more cumbersome for interviewers to use, and may take more interviewer training. But if such a form can be incorporated into the study, even the small increase in reporting that occurs could be worth the effort.

We should stress that the open-ended format that produced the large effects was limited to questions about the amount or frequency of behavior—for example, "How much liquor did you drink or how many times a week did you drink?"—and so yielded a number that was easily coded. The cost of this type of format is not substantially different from the precoded form. Our studies did not investigate the use of open-ended formats with questions involving attitudes or behavioral questions involving nonquantitative answers (for example, symptoms or complaints). Use of the open-ended format in such situations would add greatly to the coding costs. Also, it should be noted that only the answer format was open-ended and not the questions themselves.

Changes in the form of the questions do not, however, eliminate underreporting altogether. The analysis of the experiment using the three different forms revealed that the form effects were limited to reports about the quantity and frequency of behavior once respondents reported engaging in the behavior at all; the form of the questions did not influence the probability that respondents would report engaging in the behavior at all. We can think of the decision to report about threatening behaviors as a two-step process. First, the respondents decide whether or not to report that they have engaged in the type of behavior being asked about. This decision is influenced by the facts of the situation (such as whether they remember actually doing the behavior or not) and by their own feelings about whether they want to tell the interviewer about it. If the decision is negative—either because they have not in fact done anything or do not remember doing it, or because they do not want to talk about it—the series of questions is terminated. If the decision is positive, the form of the subsequent questions does play a very important role in influencing how much behavior is reported.

In this two-step process, the first step appears to be primarily determined by characteristics of the respondents, their actual behavior, and their personalities or beliefs about social norms; the second step is heavily influenced by the form of the questions. Since the first step is little influenced by the interview form, at least as far as we know, reporting errors cannot be totally eliminated by manipulations of the questionnaire format.

One potentially promising technique for circumventing respondents' reluctance to talk about threatening matters in regard to their own behavior is to ask them about the behavior of their friends. The analysis of data on questions about the behavior of the respondent's three best friends indicates that asking such questions produces some increase in reporting for threatening questions about behavior that occurred during the past year. This increase is general and seems to occur both for respondents who felt people would be very uneasy in talking about the topic (who themselves tended to report less behavior) and for those who did not think people would be made uneasy. The results were sufficiently encouraging to suggest that further work should be done using questions about friends in conjunction with questions about the respondents' own behavior.

We also investigated briefly the effects of the presence of other people during an interview. We expected that, for threatening questions, the impact of others might be substantial, since the hypothesized effects stem from our concern about the impression that respondents feel they are making on others. Of course, the effects depend on who the other persons are. In general, our data suggested that third parties present during the interview did not make much of a difference. There was some indication that the presence of a child made respondents more uneasy about discussing threatening behaviors and that the presence of adult third parties may increase the probability of refusals. But the effects were small. An intriguing hint of a possibly large effect (the sample size was too small to say anything definitive) was found in the few interviews in which young respondents were interviewed in the presence of their parents. Since generational differences were found in reports of threatening behaviors and in some attitudes, such an effect makes a good deal of sense. Further research should certainly be done to test for this effect.

Studies involving threatening topics raise questions about confidentiality and informed consent to a greater extent than do studies involving low-threat material. To what extent are respondents sensitive to differences in assurance of confidentiality or to differing degrees of effort to ensure that they are adequately informed about the content of the survey? One of our experiments involved variations in the completeness of the description of the content of the survey, in the degree of confidentiality promised, and in the requirement that the respondents give us a signed consent form.

Only the request for a signature on the consent form had any effect on the response rate for the questionnaire as a whole. But the request for a signature before the interview begins appears to have some sensitizing effect on the respondent and may reduce the validity of reports of threatening behaviors. If it is imperative that a signed consent form be obtained, it is clearly preferable that the signature be obtained after the interview is completed rather than before.

Assuring respondents of absolute confidentiality has a small but consistent effect on the willingness of respondents to answer individual threatening questions, although not on their willingness to participate in the survey or on the quality of their behavioral reports. Thus, efforts to maintain strict confidentiality do seem to be important for surveys dealing with threatening topics.

More detailed, informative, and truthful introductions to the survey questionnaire have no effect on overall response rates or on responses to individual questions. Simply informing respondents that the interview will deal with specific threatening topics does not have the same sensitizing effect that asking for a signed consent form has. Perhaps asking for the signature is viewed as excessive, since respondents have already been told that participation is voluntary and that they may refuse to answer any questions they do not want to answer. In such circumstances, asking additionally for a signed consent form may arouse suspicions that there is something in the interview even more threatening than what they have been told about.

Interviewer Effects

In face-to-face and telephone interviewing, persons other than the respondent are involved in the question asking and recording. The fact that so much of survey research is conducted through the agency of interviewers makes the interviewer as a potential source of error a subject of considerable interest. Indeed, much of the research on response effects in the early days of survey research was based on the assumption that the interviewer was the major source of error (see Hyman and others, 1954). In our review of the literature on response effects (Sudman and Bradburn, 1974), however, we found very little evidence of large interviewer effects in general when one was dealing with trained interviewers. The major situation in which there were demonstrable significant interviewer effects was in connection with questions for which a visible characteristic of the interviewer was salient. In particular, the race of the interviewer had effects on responses to attitude questions about race relations, depending on the race of the respondent. But, by and large, interviewer effects are small compared with the effects we have found for question wording.

We investigated two aspects of interviewer behavior that might affect respondents' answers to questions. The first involved direct measures of interviewer performance derived from an analysis of tape recordings of the interviewers. From these tapes, we found that interviewers do in fact frequently alter the wording of the questions as printed in the questionnaire and add words or phrases of their own. Over one third of the questions were not read exactly as written, and, somewhat surprisingly, more experienced interviewers made more reading errors.

Further analysis of interviewer behavior, however, indicates that the occurrence of considerable amounts of nonprogrammed speech on the part of the interviewers may not be a bad thing. For example, there was a relationship between the characteristics of the respondent and the amount of nonprogrammed interviewer speech. More nonprogrammed speech occurred with older respondents. This result makes sense, since older respondents give more inappropriate answers and ask more often for clarification. In addition, interviewers tended to probe more with older respondents to make sure that they understood their responses. The fact that more experienced interviewers tended to use nonprogrammed speech more often also reflects the fact that they are more likely to probe and to give feedback, which tends to promote greater rapport with the respondent and make the interview flow more freely.

There was no evidence that the occurrence of nonpro-

172 Improving Interview Method and Questionnaire Design

grammed speech affected the quality of the responses positively or negatively. It was not related to tension in the interview, nor did it appear to be more frequent in the sections of the questionnaire that included threatening questions. It would appear that interviewers use their own judgment in speaking to respondents and depart from the written questionnaire when it seems appropriate in a particular interview situation. Although the longer questions, which we found did produce better reporting, caused more actual reading errors, these errors did not have a negative effect that offset the advantages of using the longer questions with threatening topics.

It seems clear from the data in this study that trained interviewers are capable of using good judgment in adjusting their speech behavior (and almost certainly other behaviors that we were not able to observe) to fit the circumstances of specific interviews to complete the interviews successfully. Since one cannot completely standardize every aspect of the interview situation, as long as there is considerable variance among respondents, we should not expect interviewers to be completely programmed. Indeed, it is one of the virtues of good interviewers that they are flexible and can appropriately adjust their behavior and speech to the situations they find themselves in. Such flexibility is a real asset in carrying out surveys of the general population. Efforts to standardize questions should not lead to a rigidity that requires interviewers to abandon their common sense.

In addition to the direct measures of interviewer behavior from the tape recordings of interviews, we also asked interviewers who worked on the form-experiment survey to fill out a questionnaire at the beginning of the training period about their expectations of what would be easy or difficult about the study. We had hypothesized that there would be a relationship between expectations of difficulties in interviewing and actual difficulties encountered. This hypothesis was supported by the data, but the effects were not very large. Depending on the question, those interviewers who did not expect difficulties or underreporting obtained from about 5 to 30 percent higher reports of behavior in response to threatening questions.

For surveys involving threatening topics, it would be a good idea to obtain a pretraining measure of the interviewers' expectations about difficulties with threatening questions. Then either those interviewers who expect considerable difficulties should not be assigned to that study, or time should be spent in training sessions to change their expectations and teach them how to handle problems if they should arise.

Respondent Effects

Ordinarily, we would not think of respondent effects as related to nonsampling errors, because it is the differences among respondents that we are interested in. With regard to threatening behavior, however, we suspect that there will be considerable individual variation in motivated underreporting—that is, some individuals will deliberately withhold information, because they do not want to reveal it to the interviewer. Thus, in addition to real differences among respondents, there will also be some errors in reporting, because some individuals will knowingly distort their responses.

In our studies, we approached this problem in two ways. First, we tried to get respondents' perceptions of the norms regarding talking with strangers about threatening topics. We hypothesized that those respondents who felt there were norms against discussing certain topics openly with strangers would be more likely to deny that they engaged in those particular behaviors. We did find some evidence that this type of distortion might be occurring; although we do not have external validity data to support this view definitively, the evidence is consistent with such a hypothesis.

The other method we used was to investigate a test, the Marlowe-Crowne scale, which has been used in surveys to measure the tendency of individual respondents to distort their answers in a socially desirable direction. If such a test were valid, it would allow researchers to identify individuals who had a high probability of distorting their answers and to adjust the responses to take into consideration the probability that the responses were in fact not true. Although the Marlowe-Crowne scale has been used in a number of studies for this purpose, we did not feel that the evidence for its validity as a measure of response distortion was sufficiently good to adopt it uncritically. Thus, we included a short version of the scale—a version that has also been used in a number of other studies—to investigate its properties. The analysis of our data suggests that the scale is measuring something about the individual respondents, but it appears to be measuring a general trait that is related to overall behavior rather than just to a tendency to distort answers in an interview situation. The evidence by its nature cannot be definitive, because we have no external criteria for the truth of the answers, but patterns of the relationships investigated make it unlikely that the scale is measuring response effects rather than real differences among respondents. Thus, we concluded that the Marlowe-Crowne scale is not a good measure of individual response effects associated with the respondent but rather that its results should be treated as traits of the individuals and considered a part of real differences among the respondents.

Our failure to find a measure of individual response distortion, a "lie" scale if you will, should not be taken as indicating that such distortions do not occur. It seems quite likely that they do occur in many instances. But the problem of finding a method of assessing the probability that any particular respondent is distorting his or her answers is an intractable one whose answer still eludes us.

Methodological studies, by their nature, are never definitive and can only add to or supplement existing knowledge. In the experiments and studies that we have reported, we have tried to further our knowledge of response effects related to threatening questions. Although some of the results appear to be dramatic and to stand out clearly, others are less clear and need replication before they can be confidently accepted. In addition, for all our results, there is still a question of generality. To what extent are our results limited to the questions we asked? Will they apply to other threatening topics? Pending further confirmation, however, we feel that they offer some guide for researchers dealing with threatening topics and, if properly employed, can improve the quality of the data obtained.

Appendix A

Questions Used in Chicago Experiment

Chicago Community Study

1. First, we would like to know how satisfied you are with some of the main services the city is supposed to provide.
   What about the quality of public schools in Chicago—are you generally satisfied, somewhat satisfied, or very dissatisfied?
   A. Quality of public schools
   B. Parks and playgrounds for children
   C. Sports and recreation centers for teenagers
   D. Police protection
   E. Garbage collection in this neighborhood
   F. Public library facilities in the city
2. Thinking about city services like schools, parks, and garbage

collection, do you think your neighborhood gets better, about the same, or worse services than other parts of the city?

3. How long have you lived in Chicago; how many years?
   A. *IF LESS THAN ONE YEAR:* How many months?
4. How long have you lived in this neighborhood?
   A. *IF LESS THAN ONE YEAR:* How many months?
5. And how long have you lived here, at this address?
   A. *IF LESS THAN ONE YEAR:* How many months?
6. Are any of the school buildings and facilities around here used after hours for community programs or recreation?
7. Would you say the Chicago Public Library facilities in your neighborhood are good, fair, or poor?
8. There are some questions that are asked in survey research that are difficult to ask directly because many people think they are too personal. While it is understandable that people feel this way, there is a real need for the information for the population as a whole. We now have a way that makes it possible for people to give information, without telling anyone about their own situation. Let me show you how this works; we will use the next question I have here as an example. *HAND R. CARD A.* As you see, there are two questions on the card. One deals with the "real" question that the research is concerned with, the other is completely unrelated. Both questions can be answered "yes" or "no." One of the two questions is selected by chance and you answer it. (I'll show you how that works in a minute.) I do not know which question you are answering. When all the questionnaires have been tallied, the researchers can tell *how many* families have library cards, but they have no way of knowing whether any *particular* family has a library card or not.

HAND R. BOX

It is very simple, as you will see. You use this little plastic box. Notice that the box has red and blue beads in it. By shaking the box, you can get one of the beads to show in the little "window" in the bottom corner of the box. Try it. (ENCOURAGE THE R. TO "PLAY WITH" THE BOX A LITTLE, TO GET USED TO IT.) Okay. Now you'll notice that one of the questions on the card has a red circle next to it, and one has a blue circle. The question you will answer is selected by chance. Shake the box again and look at the color of the bead that shows in the window *now*—don't tell me what color it is. If the bead is blue, you answer the "blue circle" question on the card; if the bead is red, you answer the "red circle" question. I can't see which bead is in the window; and you don't tell me which question you are answering. Just tell me if your answer is "yes" or "no."

CARD A. (Red) Does anyone in your family have a library card for the Chicago Public Library? (Blue) Is your birthday in the month of January?

---

9. Now let's do that again, using the next question. *HAND R. CARD B.* Shake the box again. Look at the color of the bead in the window. Answer the question next to the color of the bead that shows in the window—red or blue. Don't tell me the question. Is your answer "yes" or "no"?

CARD B. (Red) Do you have your own Chicago Public Library Card?
(Blue) Is your birthday in the month of February?

---

10. Are there adequate recreational facilities, such as playgrounds, parks, and swimming pools, in this neighborhood?
11. Does the city have enough museums, art galleries, and public concerts?
12. Do you think the city government is doing enough to provide city services, or is it not doing enough?
13. If you had some complaint about city services and took that complaint to your alderman, would you expect him to pay a lot of attention to your complaint, some attention, very little attention, or none at all?
14. Some people don't pay much attention to local political campaigns. How about you—are you usually very interested, somewhat interested, not very interested, or not at all interested in local political campaigns in Chicago?
15. Now we are going to use the plastic box for the next question, so I won't know what your answer is.
    HAND R. CARD C AND THE BOX. Shake the box so that one of

the beads rolls into the window. Answer "yes" or "no" to the question whose color matches the color of the bead in the window.

> CARD C. (Red) Are you now a registered voter in the precinct where you live? (Blue) Is your birthday in the month of March?

16. What part of the day do you usually find most convenient to vote—before 9 a.m., between 9 a.m. and noon, between noon and 5 p.m., or after 5 p.m.?

IF NEVER VOTED (VOLUNTEERED), SKIP TO Q. 19.

17. *HAND R. CARD D AND THE BOX.* Please shake the box again, so that one of the beads rolls into the window. Answer "yes" or "no" to the question whose color matches the color of the bead in the window.

> CARD D. (Red) Did you vote in the last *primary* election—the one that took place last March? (Blue) Is your birthday in the month of April?

18. *HAND R. CARD E AND THE BOX.* Please shake the box again, and answer "yes" or "no" to the question whose color matches the color of the bead in the window.

> CARD E. (Red) Did you vote in the 1972 *Presidential* election? (Blue) Is your birthday in the month of May?

ASK EVERYONE:

19. Transportation and traffic congestion are two of the major problems of cities today. In general, would you rate Chicago's public transportation system good, fair, or poor?

20. Is the traffic noise where you live loud enough to bother you when you are inside, or is it not a problem?

21. Do you think that the Chicago Police Department does a good, fair, or poor job of controlling traffic?

22. Have you driven a car in Chicago in the last three years? IF NO, SKIP TO Q. 29.

23. In general, in the last few years, have you found it very easy, fairly easy, fairly difficult, or very difficult to get around by car in the city?

24. How is the parking around here—would you say the streets in this neighborhood are too crowded for convenient parking, or is it usually easy to park?

25. *HAND R. CARD F AND THE BOX. (LEAVE THE BOX WITH R. FOR Q'S. 25–28.)* Here is the box again. Please shake it so that one of the beads rolls into the window. Answer the question whose color matches the bead. Is your answer "yes" or "no"?

> CARD F. (Red) Have you received a ticket for parking in the last 12 months? (Blue) Is your birthday in the month of June?

26. *HAND R. CARD G.* Please shake the box again and, using this card, answer the question whose color matches the bead in the window. Is your answer "yes" or "no"?

> CARD G. (Red) Have you received a ticket for going through a red light in the past 12 months? (Blue) Is your birthday in the month of July?

27. *HAND R. CARD H.* Now shake the box again and, using this card, answer the question whose color matches the bead in the window. Is your answer "yes" or "no"?

> CARD H. (Red) During the last 12 months, have you been charged by a policeman for speeding? (Blue) Is your birthday in the month of August?

28. *HAND R. CARD I.* Now shake the box again. Use this card, and answer the question whose color matches the bead in the window. Is your answer "yes" or "no"?

> CARD I. (Red) During the last 12 months, have you been charged by a policeman for driving under the influence of liquor? (Blue) Is your birthday in the month of September?

ASK EVERYONE:

29. Would you say that, in general, people in this neighborhood are very active, moderately active, or not very active in community affairs?

30. Do you think it is safe or unsafe to walk around in this neighborhood after dark?
31. Are the streets in this neighborhood adequately lighted at night?
32. How good a job do you think the police do in protecting the lives and the property of the people in this neighborhood; would you say—a very good job, fairly good, fairly poor, or very poor?
33. Do you think the police in Chicago treat all citizens equally, or do they give some people better treatment than others?
34. The judicial court system in Chicago includes city, county, and federal courts. In general, do you feel that the courts are run efficiently?
35. Do you think that the courts treat all citizens equally, or do they give some people better treatment than others?
36. *HAND R. CARD J AND THE BOX. (LEAVE THE BOX WITH R. FOR FOUR PARTS OF Q. 36.)*
    A. Now we are going to use the box again. Please shake it so one of the beads shows in the window. Answer the question whose color matches the bead. Is your answer "yes" or "no"?

> CARD J. (Red) Have you ever been involved in a case in Probate Court? (Blue) Is your birthday in the month of October?

    B. *HAND R. CARD K.* Now shake the box again. Use this card, and answer the question whose color matches the bead in the window. Is your answer "yes" or "no"?

> CARD K. (Red) Have you ever been involved in a case in Divorce Court? (Blue) Is your birthday in the month of November?

    C. *HAND R. CARD L.* Please shake the box again, and using this card, answer the question whose color matches the bead in the window. Is your answer "yes" or "no"?

> CARD L. (Red) Have you ever been involved in a case in Small Claims Court? (Blue) Is your birthday in the month of December?

D. *HAND R. CARD M.* Please shake the box again, and using this card, answer the question whose color matches the bead in the window. Is your answer "yes" or "no"?

> CARD M. (Red) Have you ever been involved in a case in Bankruptcy Court? (Blue) Is the color of the bead in the window blue?

37. Some people believe that living in a large city affects the way people feel. *(HAND R. YELLOW SHEET AND PENCIL.)* For each of the items on this page, please answer whether it is true *for you* or false *for you.*

    A. I believe I am no more nervous than most others.
    B. I work under a great deal of pressure.
    C. I cannot keep my mind on one thing.
    D. I am more sensitive than most other people.
    E. I frequently find myself worrying about something.
    F. I am usually calm and not easily upset.
    G. I feel anxiety about something or someone almost all the time.
    H. I am happy most of the time.
    I. I have periods of such great restlessness that I cannot sit still long.
    J. I have sometimes felt that difficulties were piling up so high that I could not overcome them.
    K. I find it hard to keep my mind on a task or job.
    L. I am not unusually self-conscious.
    M. I am inclined to take things hard.
    N. Life is a strain for me much of the time.
    O. At times I think I am no good at all.
    P. I am certainly lacking in self-confidence.
    Q. I certainly feel useless at times.
    R. I am a high strung person.
    S. I sometimes feel that I am about to go to pieces.
    T. I shrink from facing a crisis or difficulty.

38. Taking things all together, how would you say things are these days—would you say you're very happy, pretty happy, or not too happy these days?

39. Are you currently—married, widowed, divorced, separated, or have you never been married?

A. *IF EVER MARRIED:* How many children have you ever had? Please count all that were born alive at any time (including any you had from a previous marriage).

40. What is the highest grade or year of regular school or college that you completed and got credit for?

41. In what year were you born?

Now a few questions about this household.

42. Is your (house/apartment) owned or being bought by you (or someone in your household), rented for cash, or occupied without payment of cash rent?

43. How about the space in this (house/apartment)—do you feel you are very crowded here, somewhat crowded, or not crowded at all?

44. How many rooms are there in this (house/apartment)? Count the kitchen, but *not* the bathrooms, halls, half-rooms (or unlived-in attics and basements).

45. How many persons *altogether* live here, related to you or not? Please include any persons who usually live here but who are away temporarily—on business, or vacation, or in a general hospital. Be sure to include babies and small children. Don't forget to include yourself in the total.

46. For the purpose of our survey, we need to have a rough indication of the income of your family. In which of these groups did your total family income, from all sources, fall last year—1971 —before taxes? Just tell me the letter of the group. *HAND R. CARD X.*

    A. Under $4,000
    B. $4,000 to $5,999
    C. $6,000 to $7,999
    D. $8,000 to $9,999
    E. $10,000 to $11,999
    F. $12,000 to $14,999
    G. $15,000 to $19,999
    H. $20,000 or over
       Refused
       Don't know

47. CODE WITHOUT ASKING *ONLY* IF THERE IS NO DOUBT IN YOUR MIND. What is your race? RECORD VERBATIM *AND* CODE.

48. Now that we are almost through with this interview, I would like to ask your feelings about it . . . Overall, would you say you enjoyed the interview very much, somewhat, or not at all?
49. Were any of the questions unclear or hard to understand?
     A. *IF YES:* Which ones?
50. Did you feel any of the questions were too personal?
     A. *IF YES:* Which ones?

Questions sometimes have different kinds of effects on people. We'd like your opinion about some of the questions in this interview.

51.   A. For example, the questions about having been involved in different kinds of court cases; do you think that those questions would make most people—very uneasy, somewhat uneasy, or not at all uneasy?
       B. Do you think the questions about court cases would *annoy* most people—very much, somewhat, or not at all?
52. *ASK ONLY PERSONS WHO HAVE DRIVEN IN CHICAGO IN LAST 3 YEARS (YES TO Q. 22):*
       A. Do you think the questions about traffic violations would make most people—very uneasy, somewhat uneasy, or not at all uneasy?
       B. Do you think the questions about traffic violations would annoy most people—very much, somewhat, or not at all?
53.   A. How about the questions on voting—do you think they would make most people very uneasy, somewhat uneasy, or not at all uneasy?
       B. Do you think the voting questions would annoy most people—very much, somewhat, or not at all?
54. And the questions about having a library card—do you think those questions would make most people very uneasy, somewhat uneasy, or not at all uneasy?
55. Finally, did any of the questions make *you* feel uneasy at all?
     A. *IF YES:* Which ones?

Thank you very much for your time and help.

56. *IF YOU DON'T ALREADY HAVE PHONE NUMBER, ASK:* May I have your telephone number just in case my office wants to verify this interview? *IF TELEPHONE NUMBER IS GIVEN, ASK A:*
     A. Is this phone located in your own home?

Thank you.

Interviewer Remarks

Complete as soon as possible after interview is completed

A. Length of interview (in minutes):
B. Date of interview:
C. Sex of respondent:
D. In general, what was the respondent's attitude toward the interview? [Friendly; Cooperative but not particularly friendly; Indifferent and bored; Nervous, uneasy; Suspicious, hostile; Other (SPECIFY).]
E. Was the respondent suspicious, hostile, nervous, or uneasy at any *particular parts* of the interview?
   [1] *IF YES:* Describe what parts or give question numbers.
F. Do you think the respondent understood the use of the Random Response Box?
G. Do you think the respondent accepted the explanation of the Box and believed that his/her answers really were private?

Appendix B

Questions Used in Nationwide Experiment

Leisure Activity Study

This survey is about how people are feeling in general and about the kinds of activities people do in their leisure time—that is, their spare time when they are not working.

Some of the questions in this survey may be hard to answer, or make you feel uneasy. There are questions about your moods, and about the time you spend watching television or going to sports events, about your social activities, and some about your use of alcoholic drinks and drugs. We also ask a few questions about sex. If you feel uneasy about answering a question, you need not answer it, and we will go on to the next question. If you do help us by answering a question, please be as truthful and as accurate as you can.

1. First, I'd like to get a general idea about the specific kinds of things you do for recreation or to relax. I have a list of activities people sometimes do. Please think back *over the past month.* As I read each activity, please tell me whether or not you have done it this past month. Did you:
    a. Go to a movie?
    b. Dine at a restaurant for pleasure?
    c. Go window shopping?
    d. Go to a theater or concert?
    e. Go on a picnic?
    f. Go hunting or fishing?
    g. Read for pleasure?
    h. Take a ride in an automobile for pleasure?
    i. Do gardening for pleasure?
    j. Participate in a civic or religious organization or club?
    k. Go for a walk or a hike?
    l. Go to a professional, college, or high school sports event?
2. Now, I have some questions about sports. Please think back *over the past year.* Did you:
    a. Play badminton?
    b. Play basketball?
    c. Go bowling?
    d. Play football?
    e. Play golf?
    f. Play racketball, handball, paddleball or squash?
    g. Play softball or baseball?
    h. Swim?
    i. Play tennis?
3. In the last week, about how many hours a day did you watch television?
4. About how many hours a day did you listen to the radio?
5. And about how many hours a day did you listen to records or tapes?
6. In general, how important to you are the activities which you do in your leisure time or for recreation? Are they very important, moderately important, slightly important, or not at all important?

During the interview, I will give you cards with possible answers to some of the questions. Just look over the card and tell me which answer comes closest to the right answer for you. *HAND R. CARD A.*

7. How satisfied are you with the things you do in your leisure time or for recreation? Are you completely satisfied, very satisfied, moderately satisfied, slightly satisfied, or not at all satisfied?

We'd like to know some things about living here.

8. All in all, how satisfied are you with living in this (house/apartment)? Are you completely satisfied, very satisfied, moderately satisfied, slightly satisfied, or not at all satisfied?

9. Taking everything into account, how do you feel about living in this (neighborhood/IN RURAL AREAS: area)? Are you completely satisfied, very satisfied, moderately satisfied, slightly satisfied, or not at all satisfied?

We are interested in how people are getting along financially these days.

10. As far as you and your family are concerned, would you say that you are completely satisfied with your present financial situation, very satisfied, moderately satisfied, slightly satisfied, or not at all satisfied?

11. Generally speaking, how satisfied would you say you are with your life as a whole—completely satisfied, very satisfied, moderately satisfied, slightly satisfied, or not at all satisfied?

12. What is your marital status? Are you married, divorced, separated, widowed, or have you never been married?

13. *HAND R. CARD B.* IF RESPONDENT IS NOT MARRIED, GO TO Q. 14. How would you describe your marriage, taking all things together? Would you say your marriage is completely happy, very happy, moderately happy, slightly happy, or not at all happy?

14. Would you say your own health, in general, is excellent, good, fair, or poor?

15. Taken all together, how would you say things are these days? Would you say that you are completely happy, very happy, moderately happy, slightly happy, or not at all happy?

16. *HAND R. CARD C.* We are interested in the way people are feeling these days. During the past few weeks, how often did you feel:

      a. particularly excited or interested in something?

      b. so restless that you couldn't sit still long?

    c. proud because someone complimented you on some-
thing you had done?

    d. very lonely or remote from people?

    e. pleased about having accomplished something?

    f. bored?

    g. on top of the world?

    h. depressed or very unhappy?

    i. that things were going your way?

    j. upset because someone had criticized you?

17. REFER TO RESPONSE Q. 16a ABOVE. IF "NEVER" GO
TO Q. 18. When you said that you felt particularly excited or
interested in something (REPEAT RESPONDENT'S AN-
SWER TO a)—about how many times a week or a month did
you mean?

18. REFER TO RESPONSE TO Q. 16f ABOVE. IF "NEVER" GO
TO Q. 19. When you said that you felt bored (REPEAT RE-
SPONDENT'S ANSWER TO f)—about how many times a
week or a month did you mean?

19. *HAND R. CARD D.* Listed on this card are a number of statements concerning personal attitudes and traits. Read each
item and decide whether the statement is true or false as it pertains to you personally.

    a. Before voting, I thoroughly investigate the qualifi-
cations of all the candidates.

    b. I never hesitate to go out of my way to help someone
in trouble.

    c. On occasion, I have had doubts about my ability to
succeed in life.

    d. If I could get into a movie without paying for it and be
sure I was not seen, I would probably do it.

    e. There have been times when I felt like rebelling
against people in authority even though I knew they
were right.

    f. No matter who I'm talking to, I'm always a good
listener.

    g. I sometimes try to get even, rather than forgive and
forget.

    h. At times I have really insisted on having things my
own way.

      i. I never resent being asked to return a favor.

      j. I have never been irked when people expressed ideas very different from my own.

20. I am going to read you some things that many people like to do with friends in their leisure time. Would you tell me whether you have done any of these things with any of your friends during the past year?

    a. People often bet on card games while playing at home on some card night, while playing with friends in a lounge, and in similar situations. Have you played poker, blackjack or 21, bridge, pinochle, or any other card games for money?

    b. People also bet with friends on who wins or loses some sporting event. Not including betting pools, have you bet on a sporting event such as a football, baseball or basketball game?

    c. Although the presidential election was more than two years ago, some people bet on other elections or on contests. Have you bet with friends on some other event such as the outcome of an election or the winner of a contest?

    d. People often participate in betting pools with fellow workers, with fellow members of a club or organization, or with other friends. In the past year, have you participated in a betting pool?

    e. Dice games always have been a popular way for people to gamble with friends. Have you rolled dice, shot craps, or played other dice games for money?

21. Many states now conduct lotteries to earn money for the state treasury. In fact, thirteen states currently are licensed to conduct public lotteries, with prizes ranging as high as one million dollars. Have you bought a state lottery ticket within the past year?

22. We have some questions about various kinds of social activities—things such as giving parties, spending social evenings with relatives or friends, or going out to a tavern or bar. As I read each type of social activity, please tell me how often you have done it during the past year.

    a. Given a party for 5 or more people?

   b. Gone to a bar, tavern, or lounge?
   c. Spent a social evening with relatives?
   d. Spent a social evening with friends who live in your (neighborhood/IN RURAL AREAS: area)?
   e. Spent a social evening with friends who live outside your (neighborhood/IN RURAL AREAS: area)?

Now we have some questions about drinking for relaxation.

23. The most popular alcoholic beverage in this country is beer or ale. People drink beer in taverns, with meals, in pizza parlors, at sporting events, at home while watching television, and many other places. Did you *ever* drink, even once, beer or ale? IF NO, GO TO Q. 24.

   A. *IF YES:* We are especially interested in recent times. Have you drunk any beer or ale in the past year? IF YES, ASK (1), (2), AND (3). IF NO, ASK (1) AND (2).

   (1) When you drank beer or ale, on the average, how often did you drink it? Include every time you drank it, no matter how little you had.

   (2) Most of the times you drank beer, on the average, about how many bottles, cans or glasses did you drink at one time?

   (3) *ASK IF R. HAS DRUNK IN PAST YEAR:* Thinking about more recent times, have you drunk any beer or ale in the past month?

24. Wines have become increasingly popular in this country over the last few years; by wines, we mean liqueurs, cordials, sherries, and similar drinks, as well as table wines, sparkling wines, and champagne. Did you *ever* drink, even once, wine or champagne? IF NO, GO TO Q. 25.

   A. *IF YES:* You might have drunk wine to build your appetite before dinner, to accompany dinner, to celebrate some occasion, to enjoy a party, or for some other reason. Have you drunk any wine or champagne in the past year? IF YES, ASK (1), (2), and (3). IF NO, ASK (1) AND (2).

   (1) When you drank wine or champagne, on the average how often did you drink it? Include every time you drank it, no matter how little you had.

(2) Most of the times you drank wine or champagne, on the average about how many glasses did you drink at one time?

(3) *IF R. HAS DRUNK IN PAST YEAR:* Thinking about more recent times than the past year, have you drunk any wine or champagne in the past month?

F (25). Part of our research is to try to find out the best way to ask questions. Sometimes as we go through the questionnaire, I'll ask you to suggest terms that we might use so that you will feel comfortable and understand what we mean. For instance, my next few questions are about all the drinks like whiskey, vodka, and gin. What do you think would be the best thing to call all the beverages of that kind when we ask questions about them?

IF NO RESPONSE, OR AWKWARD PHRASE, USE "LIQUOR" IN FOLLOWING QUESTIONS. OTHERWISE, USE RESPONDENT'S WORD(S).

25. People drink _____ by itself or with mixers such as water, soft drinks, juices and liqueurs. Did you ever drink, even once, _____ ? IF NO, GO TO Q. F (26).

A. *IF YES:* You might have drunk _____ as a cocktail, appetizer, to relax in a bar, to celebrate some occasion, to enjoy a party, or for some other reason. Have you drunk any _____ in the past year? IF YES, ASK (1), (2), AND (3). IF NO, ASK (1) AND (2).

(1) When you drank _____, on the average how often did you drink it? Include every time you drank it, no matter how little you had.

(2) Most of the times you drank _____, on the average about how many drinks did you have at one time?

(3) *IF R. HAS DRUNK IN PAST YEAR:* Thinking about more recent times than the past year, have you drunk any _____ in the past month?

F (26). Sometimes people drink a little too much beer, wine, or whiskey so that they act different from usual. What word do you think we should use to describe people when they get that way, so that you will know what we mean and feel comfortable talking about it?

IF NO RESPONSE, OR AWKWARD PHRASE, USE "IN-TOXICATED" IN FOLLOWING QUESTIONS. OTH-ERWISE, USE RESPONDENT'S WORD(S).

26. *IF R. HAS ANSWERED YES FOR DRINKING ANY ALCOHOL IN THE PAST YEAR:* Occasionally, people drink on an empty stomach or drink a little too much and become _____. In the past year, how often did you become _____ while drinking any kind of alcoholic beverage?

27. Next, think of your three closest friends. Don't mention their names, just get them in mind. As far as you know, how many of them have been _____ during the past year?

F (28). Different people use different words for marijuana or hashish. What do you think we should call them so you understand us?

IF NO RESPONSE, OR AWKWARD PHRASE, USE "MARIJUANA" IN FOLLOWING QUESTIONS. OTH-ERWISE, USE RESPONDENT'S WORD(S).

28. _____ is commonly used. People smoke _____ in private to relax, with friends at parties, with friends to relax, and in other situations. Have you, yourself, at any time in your life smoked _____ ? IF YES, ASK B, C, AND D. IF NO, ASK A.

IF NO:

A. Not at all, not even just once? IF YES, ASK B, C, AND D. IF NO, GO TO Q. 29.

IF YES:

B. To put things in a recent time frame, have you smoked _____ during the past year? IF YES, ASK (1). IF NO, GO TO C.

(1) *IF YES TO B:* Have you smoked _____ during the past month?

C. Counting every time you smoked _____, no matter how little you used, has there ever been a time when you were smoking it at least three times a week? IF YES, ASK (1). IF NO, GO TO D.

(1) *IF YES TO C:* About how many weeks did that time last? (IF THERE HAS BEEN MORE THAN ONE TIME, ASK FOR THE LONGEST TIME.)

D. When you smoked _____, how many cigarettes or pipes did you usually smoke on an average day? (IF

SHARED WITH FRIENDS: How many cigarettes would your share amount to?)

29. Think of your three closest friends again. (Don't mention their names.) As far as you know, how many of them have ever smoked _____ ?

　A. *IF ANY EVER SMOKED:* And how many would you say smoked _____ during the past year?

F (30). *HAND R. CARD N.* Here is a list of drug names. Some of these are different common names for amphetamines, and others are stimulant drugs that have effects somewhat like amphetamines. What word would you suggest we use in talking about these drugs?

IF NO RESPONSE, OR AWKWARD PHRASE, USE "STIMULANTS" IN FOLLOWING QUESTIONS. OTHERWISE, USE RESPONDENT'S WORD(S).

30. Doctors often prescribe _____ for medical purposes. In addition, people sometimes take these drugs without a prescription or take more than their prescription indicates, for medical and non-medical reasons.

Look over the list and tell me, at any time in your life, have you ever taken any _____ without a prescription or *more* than prescribed? IF YES, ASK B, C, AND D. IF NO, ASK A.

IF NO:

　A. Not at all, not even just once? IF YES, ASK B, C, AND D. IF NO, GO TO Q. F (31).

IF YES:

　B. To put things in a recent time frame, have you taken any of these drugs without a prescription in the past year? IF YES, ASK (1). IF NO, GO TO C.

　　(1) IF YES TO B: Have you taken any of these drugs during the past month?

　C. Some of the specific reasons people give for using_____ are to lose weight, to stay awake, to get high, to perform better, and to see what they are like. Have you ever used them to get high, or did you always use them for some other reason? IF TO GET HIGH, ASK (1). IF FOR SOME OTHER REASON, SPECIFY AND GO TO Q. F (31).

　　(1) *IF TO GET HIGH:* Counting every time you used

_____ to get high, no matter how small an amount you took, has there been at least a month when you've taken them twice a week or more not on prescription? IF YES, ASK

a. IF NO, GO TO D.

a. *IF YES TO (1):* About how many weeks did that time last? (IF MORE THAN ONE TIME, ASK FOR THE LONGEST TIME.)

D. We're interested in the amount of money spent on _____ , as well as how frequently they are used. When you used _____ , about how much money did you usually spend a week on them? (PROBE: In an average week?)

F (31). *HAND R. CARD P.* Here is another list of drug names. What word do you suggest we use when talking about these drugs?

IF NO RESPONSE, OR AWKWARD PHRASE, USE "SEDATIVES" IN THE FOLLOWING QUESTIONS. OTHERWISE, USE RESPONDENT'S WORD(S).

31. Doctors also prescribe _____ for medical purposes. In addition, people sometimes take these drugs without a prescription or take more than their prescription indicates, for several different medical and non-medical reasons.

    Look over the list and tell me, at any time in your life, have you taken any _____ without a prescription, or more than was prescribed? IF YES, ASK B, C, AND D. IF NO, ASK A.

    IF NO:

    A. Not at all, not even just once? IF YES, ASK B, C, AND D. IF NO, GO TO Q. 32.

    IF YES:

    B. To put things in a recent time frame, have you taken any of these drugs without a prescription in the past year? IF YES, ASK (1). IF NO, GO TO C.

    (1) *IF YES TO B:* Have you taken any of these drugs during the past month?

    C. Some of the specific reasons people give for using _____ are to enjoy their effects, to come down from uppers, to ease physical pain, to sleep, to calm their nerves, and to see what they are like. Have you ever used them to enjoy their effects, or did you always use them for some other reason? IF TO ENJOY EFFECTS, ASK (1). IF FOR SOME OTHER REASON, SPECIFY AND GO TO Q. 32.

(1) *IF TO ENJOY EFFECTS IN C:* Counting every time you used _____ to enjoy their effects, no matter how small an amount you used, has there been a time when you've taken them several days a week—not on prescription, or without a doctor's okay? IF YES, ASK

a. IF NO, GO TO D.

a. *IF YES TO (1):* About how many weeks did that time last? (IF MORE THAN ONE TIME, ASK FOR THE LONGEST TIME.)

D. We're interested in the amount of money spent on _____ , as well as how frequently they are used. When you used _____ , about how much money did you usually spend a week on them? (PROBE: In an average week?)

Now we have some questions about sexual activity.

32. Many people used to feel that petting or kissing were private matters that never should be talked about. However, most people these days are willing to answer questions about this type of activity. In the past month, have you engaged in petting or kissing? IF YES, ASK A AND B. IF NO OR PREFER NOT TO ANSWER, GO TO Q. F (33).

IF YES:

A. People are very different in how often they engage in this type of activity—anywhere from once a month or less to almost every day or more. On the average, how often did you engage in petting or kissing during the month?

B. Thinking about a more recent period than the past month, have you engaged in petting or kissing during the past 24 hours?

F (33). Different people use different words for sexual intercourse. What word do you think we should use?

IF NO RESPONSE, OR AWKWARD PHRASE, USE

"INTERCOURSE" IN FOLLOWING QUESTIONS. OTHERWISE, USE RESPONDENT'S WORD(S).

33. Although most people are willing to talk about petting or kissing, some people may still feel uncomfortable answering questions about _____. Other people aren't uncomfortable talking about _____. In the past month, have you (engaged in) _____? IF YES, ASK A AND B. IF NO OR PREFER NOT TO ANSWER, GO TO Q. F (34).

    IF YES:

    A. People also are very different in how often they (engage in) _____ —anywhere from once a month or less to almost every day or more. On the average, how often did you (engage in) _____ during the month?

    B. Thinking about a more recent period than the past month, have you (engaged in) _____ during the past 24 hours?

F (34). Another form of sexual activity is masturbation, in which persons sexually stimulate themselves. What words do you think we should use to refer to this activity?

IF NO RESPONSE, OR AWKWARD PHRASE, USE "MASTURBATION" IN FOLLOWING QUESTIONS. OTHERWISE, USE RESPONDENT'S WORD(S).

34. Past studies have found _____ to be almost as common as sexual activity between people, such as petting and kissing. In the past month, have you _____? IF YES, ASK A AND B. IF NO OR PREFER NOT TO ANSWER, GO TO Q. 35.

    IF YES:

    A. As with sexual activity between persons, people are very different in how often they _____ —anywhere from once a month or less to almost every day or more. On the average, how often did you _____ during the past month?

    B. Thinking about a more recent period than the past month, did you _____ during the past 24 hours?

Now, a few background items for statistical tabulation purposes only. Remember, at no time will any of this information be used to identify anyone.

35. In what year were you born?

36. INTERVIEWER: CODE—*DO NOT ASK*—SEX OF RESPON-DENT.
37. Are you currently employed? IF YES, ASK A, B, C, AND D. IF NO, GO TO Q. 38.
    IF YES:
    A. What is your main occupation or job title?
    B. What kind of work do you do, that is, what are your duties on this job?
    C. In what type of business or industry is this, that is, what product is made or what service is given?
    D. (*RECORD ON CARD A.*) On the whole, how satisfied are you with the work you do—would you say you are completely satisfied, very satisfied, moderately satisfied, slightly satisfied, or not at all satisfied?
38. *IF CURRENTLY MARRIED (Q. 12):* Is your (husband/wife) currently employed? IF YES, ASK A, B, AND C. IF NO, GO TO Q. 39.
    IF YES:
    A. What is (his/her) main occupation or job title?
    B. What kind of work does (he/she) do, that is, what are (his/her) duties on this job?
    C. In what type of business or industry is this, that is, what product is made or what service is given?
39. What is the highest grade of regular school that you ever attended?
ASK Q. 40 IF R. IS MARRIED, SEPARATED OR WIDOWED (Q. 12). ALL OTHERS SKIP TO Q. 41.
40. What is the highest grade of regular school that your (husband/wife) ever attended?
41. INTERVIEWER: *CODE WITHOUT ASKING:* IS THIS A HOUSE OR AN APARTMENT?
42. *ASK:* Do you own or rent this (house/apartment)? SPECIFY IF OTHER ARRANGEMENT.
43. Some people hesitate to answer survey questions about their income, because they don't want other people to know how much they make or because they're afraid that the Internal Revenue Service will get the information. Actually, as with *all* answers in this survey, this information is strictly confiden-

tial. We ask the question only because people's income seems to influence their leisure activities, and thus we don't even need an exact amount, but only an estimate. What was your *total family* income before taxes in 1974?

44. INTERVIEWER: CODE—*DO NOT ASK*—RACE OF RE-SPONDENT.
    a. White
    b. Black
    c. Oriental
    d. Spanish-American
    e. Other (SPECIFY)

45. Now that we are almost through with this interview, I would like your feelings about it. Overall, how enjoyable was this interview?

46. Which questions, if any, were unclear or hard to understand?

47. Which of the questions, if any, were too personal?

48. *HAND R. CARD W.* Questions sometimes have different kinds of effects on people. We'd like your opinions about some of the questions in this interview. As I mention groups of questions, please tell me whether you think those questions would make *most people* very uneasy, moderately uneasy, slightly uneasy, or not at all uneasy.

    How about the questions on:
    a. Leisure time and general leisure activities?
    b. Sport activities?
    c. Happiness and well-being?
    d. Gambling with friends?
    e. Social activities?
    f. Drinking beer, wine or liquor?
    g. Getting drunk?
    h. Using marijuana or hashish?
    i. Using stimulants or depressants?
    j. Petting or kissing?
    k. Intercourse?
    l. Masturbation?
    m. Occupation?
    n. Education?
    o. Income?
    p. How about the use of the tape recorder?

Thank you very much for your time and help.

49. May I have your telephone number just in case my office wants to verify this interview?

    A. *IF NUMBER IS GIVEN:* Is this phone located in your own home?

50. Did asking for your telephone number make you feel slightly uneasy?

Thank you very much for your time and cooperation. These are all the questions I have.

Interviewer Remarks

Complete as soon as possible after interview is completed

1. Was the respondent very cooperative, somewhat cooperative, or not cooperative?

    A. *IF NOT COOPERATIVE:* What seemed to be the trouble?

2. Did the respondent seem to enjoy the interview?

3. Was anyone else present during any part of the interview?
   IF YES:

    A. Who was it?
   Spouse; Child; Parent; Sibling; Other (SPECIFY).

    B. During which parts of the interview was someone else present? SPECIFY WHO IN WHICH PARTS.

4. Were there any questions which the respondent did not seem to understand?

    A. *IF YES:* Which ones?

5. Do you feel the respondent was honest with you, even when (he/she) felt uneasy about answering?

6. Disregarding the respondent's answers, were there any groups of questions which *you* felt caused at least some difficulty during the interview?

    a. Happiness and well-being

    b. Gambling with friends

    c. Social activities

    d. Drinking beer, wine or liquor

    e. Getting drunk

    f. Using marijuana or hashish

    g. Using stimulants or depressants

    h. Petting and kissing

    i. Intercourse

        j . Masturbation
        k . Occupation
        l . Education
        m. Income
        n . Use of tape recorder
        o . Phone number

7. Was the interview taped?
   IF YES:
     A. WRITE QUESTIONNAIRE NUMBER ON THE TAPE LABEL.
     B. "FAST FORWARD" TAPE TO END.
   IF NO:
     C. Why wasn't the interview taped?
8. Date of interview
9. Length of interview (in minutes)

References

Abelson, H. I., and Atkinson, R. B. *Public Experience with Psychoactive Substances.* Prepared for the National Institute on Drug Abuse. Princeton, N.J.: Response Analysis Corporation, 1975.

Alexander, S., and Husek, T. "The Anxiety Differential: Initial Steps in the Development of a Measure of Situational Anxiety." *Educational and Psychological Measurement,* 1965, *22,* 325–348.

Aronson, E., and Carlsmith, J. M. "Experimentation in Social Psychology." In G. Lindzey and E. Aronson (Eds.), *Handbook of Social Psychology.* Vol. 2 (2nd ed.). Reading, Mass.: Addison-Wesley, 1968.

Ash, P., and Abramson, E. "The Effect of Anonymity on Attitude Questionnaire Response." *Journal of Abnormal and Social Psychology,* 1952, *47,* 722–723.

Barber, B. "Experimentation with Human Beings: Another Problem of Civil Rights?" *Minerva,* 1973, *2,* 415–419.

Bass, B. M., Cascio, W. F., and O'Connor, E. J. "Magnitude Estimations of Expressions of Frequency and Amount." *Journal of Applied Psychology,* 1974, *59,* 313–320.

Belson, W. A. "Tape Recording: Its Effect on Accuracy of Response in Survey Interviews." *Journal of Marketing Research,* 1967, *4,* 253–260.

Bendig, A. W. "The Development of a Short Form of the Manifest Anxiety Scale." *Journal of Consulting Psychology,* 1956, *20,* 384.

Blumberg, H., Fuller, C., and Hare, A. P. "Response Rates in Postal Surveys." *Public Opinion Quarterly,* 1974, *38,* 113–123.

Bradburn, N. M. *The Structure of Psychological Well-Being.* Chicago: Aldine, 1969.

Bucher, R., Fritz, C. E., and Quarantelli, E. L. "Tape Recorded Interviews in Social Research." *American Sociological Review,* 1956, *21,* 359–364.

Bureau of Agricultural Economics, Division of Program Surveys. *Veterans' Readjustment to Civilian Life.* Washington, D.C.: Department of Agriculture, 1945.

Campbell, A., Converse, P., and Rodgers, W. *The Quality of American Life: Perceptions, Evaluations, and Satisfactions.* New York: Russell Sage Foundation, 1976.

Cannell, C. F., and Kahn, R. "Interviewing." In G. Lindzey and E. Aronson (Eds.), *Handbook of Social Psychology.* Vol. 2 (2nd ed.). Reading, Mass.: Addison-Wesley, 1968.

Cannell, C. F., Lawson, S. A., and Hausser, D. L. *A Technique for Evaluating Interviewer Performance.* Ann Arbor, Mich.: Institute for Social Research, 1975.

Chase, C. I. "Often Is Where You Find It." *American Psychologist,* 1969, *24,* 1043.

Clancy, K. J. "Systematic Bias in Field Studies of Mental Illness." Unpublished doctoral dissertation, Department of Sociology, New York University, 1971.

Clancy, K. J., and Gove, W. "Sex Differences in Respondents' Reports of Psychiatric Symptoms: An Analysis of Response Bias." *American Journal of Sociology,* 1974, *80,* 205–216.

Clark, A. L., and Wallin, P. "The Accuracy of Husbands' and Wives' Reports of Frequency of Marital Coitus." *Population Studies,* 1964, *18,* 165–173.

Cliff, N. "Adverbs as Multipliers." *Psychological Review,* 1959, *66,* 27–44.

Colombotos, J. "Personal Versus Telephone Interviews: Effects on Responses." *Public Health Reports,* 1969, *84,* 773–782.

Conn, L. K., and Crowne, D. "Instigation to Aggression, Emotional Arousal and Defensive Emulation." *Journal of Personality,* 1964, *32,* 163–179.

Crowne, D. P., and Marlowe, D. "A New Scale of Social Desirability Independent of Psychopathology." *Journal of Consulting Psychology,* 1960, *24,* 349–354.

Crowne, D. P., and Marlowe, D. *The Approval Motive: Studies in Evaluative Dependence.* New York: Wiley, 1964.

DeLamater, J., and MacCorquodale, P. "The Effects of Interview Schedule Variations on Reported Sexual Behavior." *Sociological Methods and Research,* 1975, *4,* 215–236.

Engel, J. F. "Tape Recorders in Consumer Research." *Journal of Marketing,* 1962, *26,* 73–74.

Enterline, P. E., and Capt, K. G. "A Validation of Information Provided by Household Respondents in Health Surveys." *American Journal of Public Health,* 1959, *49,* 205–212.

Erdos, P., and Regir, J. "Visible and Disguised Keying on Questionnaires." *Journal of Advertising Research,* 1977, *17,* 13–18.

Fischer, R. P. "Signed Versus Unsigned Personal Questionnaires." *Journal of Applied Psychology,* 1946, *30,* 220–225.

Fishman, C. G. "Need for Approval and the Expression of Aggression Under Varying Conditions of Frustration." *Journal of Personality and Social Psychology,* 1965, *2,* 809–816.

Fuller, C. "Effect of Anonymity on Return Rate and Response Bias in a Mail Survey." *Journal of Applied Psychology,* 1974, *59,* 292–296.

Gallup, G. *The Gallup Poll.* Princeton, N.J.: The Gallup Organization, February 14, 1977.

Gergen, K., and Marlowe, D. *Personality and Social Behavior.* Reading, Mass.: Addison-Wesley, 1970.

Goocher, B. E. "Effects of Attitude and Experience on the Selection of Frequency Adverbs." *Journal of Verbal Learning and Verbal Behavior,* 1965, *4,* 193–195.

Gorsuch, R. "Changes in Trait Anxiety as a Function of Recent States of Anxiety." *Proceedings of the American Statistical Association.* Washington, D.C.: American Statistical Association, 1969.

Gove, W. R., and Geerken, M. R. "Response Bias in Surveys of Mental Health: An Empirical Investigation." *American Journal of Sociology,* 1977, *82,* 1289–1317.

Gray, B. H. *Human Subjects in Medical Experimentation.* New York: Wiley, 1975.

Greenberg, B., and others. "The Unrelated Question Randomized Response Model: Theoretical Framework." *Journal of the American Statistical Association,* 1969, *64,* 520–539.

Hakel, M. D. "How Often Is Often?" *American Psychologist,* 1968, *23,* 533–534.

Hanson, R., and Marks, E. "Influence of the Interviewer on the Accuracy of Survey Results." *Journal of the American Statistical Association,* 1958, *53,* 635–655.

Harris, L., and Associates, Inc. *Public Awareness of the NIAAA Advertising Campaign and Public Attitudes Toward Drinking and Alcohol Abuse.* Prepared for the National Institute on Alcohol Abuse and Alcoholism. New York: Louis Harris and Associates, 1974.

Hauck, M., and Cox, M. "Locating a Sample by Random Digit Dialing." *Public Opinion Quarterly,* 1974, *38,* 253–256.

Helson, H. *Adaptation Level Theory.* New York: Harper & Row, 1964.

Heybee, K. "Fifteen Years of Fear Research." *Psychological Bulletin,* 1969, *72,* 426–444.

Hochstim, J. R. "A Critical Comparison of Three Strategies of Collecting Data from Households." *Journal of the American Statistical Association,* 1967, *62,* 976–989.

Hodges, W., and Felling, J. "Types of Stressful Situations and Their Relation to Trait Anxiety and Sex." *Journal of Consulting and Clinical Psychology,* 1970, *34,* 333–337.

Horowitz, D. G., Shah, B. V., and Simmons, W. R. "The Unrelated Question Randomized Response Model." *Proceedings of the American Statistical Association.* Washington, D.C.: American Statistical Association, 1967.

Hyman, H., and others. *Interviewing in Social Research.* Chicago: University of Chicago Press, 1954.

Jones, L. V., and Thurstone, L. L. "The Psychophysics of Semantics: An Experimental Investigation." *Journal of Applied Psychology,* 1955, *39,* 31–36.

Jourard, S. M. *The Transparent Self.* New York: D. Van Nostrand, 1964.

Jourard, S. M. *Disclosing Man to Himself.* New York: D. Van Nostrand, 1968.

Jourard, S. M., and Friedman, R. "Experimenter-Subject 'Distance' and Self-Disclosure." *Journal of Personality and Social Psychology,* 1970, *15,* 278–282.

King, F. W. "Anonymous Versus Identifiable Questionnaires in Drug Usage Surveys." *American Psychologist,* 1970, *25,* 982–985.

Kinsey, A. C., Pomeroy, W. B., and Martin, C. E. *Sexual Behavior in the Human Male.* Philadelphia: Saunders, 1948.

Kinsey, A. C., and others. *Sexual Behavior in the Human Female.* Philadelphia: Saunders, 1953.

Kirk, R. E. *Experimental Design: Procedures for the Behavioral Sciences.* Monterey, Calif.: Brooks/Cole, 1968.

Kruskal, W. H. "Tests of Significance." In D. Sills (Ed.), *International Encyclopedia of the Social Sciences.* Vol. 14. New York: Macmillan and the Free Press, 1968.

Leibler, S. "An Analysis of Some Characteristics of Respondents and Nonrespondents to Two Mailed Questionnaires." Unpublished doctoral dissertation, Department of Education, University of Rochester, 1967.

Maccoby, E. E., and Maccoby, N. "The Interview: A Tool of Social Science." In G. Lindzey (Ed.), *Handbook of Social Psychology.* Vol. 1. Reading, Mass.: Addison-Wesley, 1954.

Miller, D., and Hewgill, M. "Some Recent Research on Fear Arousing Message Appeals." *Speech Monographs,* 1966, *33,* 371–391.

Mitchell, W., Jr. "Factors Affecting the Rates of Return on Mailed Questionnaires." *American Statistical Association Journal,* 1939, *34,* 683–692.

Mosier, C. I. "A Psychometric Study of Meaning." *Journal of Social Psychology,* 1941, *13,* 123–140.

Nejelski, P. (Ed.). *Social Research in Conflict with Law and Ethics.* Cambridge, Mass.: Ballinger, 1976.

Nie, N. H., and others. *SPSS: Statistical Package for the Social Sciences.* (2nd ed.) New York: McGraw-Hill, 1975.

Office of Substance Abuse Services. *Alcohol and Other Drug Use and Abuse in the State of Michigan.* Lansing: Michigan Department of Public Health, 1975.

Parducci, A. "Often Is Often." *American Psychologist,* 1968, *23,* 828.

Pepper, S., and Prytulak, L. S. "Sometimes Frequently Means Seldom: Context Effects in the Interpretation of Quantitative Expressions." *Journal of Research in Personality,* 1974, *8,* 95–101.

Reinmuth, J. E., and Geurts, M. D. "The Collection of Sensitive

Information Using a Two-Stage, Randomized Response Model." *Journal of Marketing Research,* 1975, *12,* 402–407.

Rosenthal, R. *Experimenter Effects in Behavior Research.* New York: Appleton-Century-Crofts, 1966.

Sarason, I. G. "Relationships of Measures of Anxiety and Experimental Instructions to Word Association Test Performance." *Journal of Abnormal and Social Psychology,* 1959, *59,* 37–42.

Simpson, R. H. "The Specific Meanings of Certain Terms Indicating Differing Degrees of Frequency." *Quarterly Journal of Speech,* 1944, *30,* 328–330.

Smith, D. H. "Correcting for Social Desirability Response Sets in Opinion-Attitude Survey Research." *Public Opinion Quarterly,* 1967, *31,* 87–94.

Smith, H., and Hyman, H. "The Biasing Effects of Interviewer Expectations on Survey Results." *Public Opinion Quarterly,* 1950, *14,* 491–506.

Spielberger, C. "Current Trends in Theory and Research on Anxiety." In C. Spielberger (Ed.), *Anxiety.* Vol. 1. New York: Academic Press, 1972.

Stouffer, S. A., and others. *The American Soldier: Combat and Its Aftermath.* Vol. 2. Princeton, N.J.: Princeton University Press, 1949.

Strahan, R., and Strahan, C. "Nature of the Marlowe-Crowne Social Desirability Variable." *Proceedings, 80th Annual Convention, American Psychological Association.* Washington, D.C.: American Psychological Association, 1972.

Strickland, L. H., and Lewicki, R. J. "Need for Social Approval and Evaluation of Military Deportment." *Journal of Consulting Psychology,* 1966, *30,* 462.

Suchman, E. A., and Phillips, B. S. "An Analysis of the Validity of Health Questionnaires." *Social Forces,* 1958, *36,* 223–232.

Sudman, S. *Applied Sampling.* New York: Academic Press, 1976.

Sudman, S., and Bradburn, N. M. *Response Effects in Surveys: A Review and Synthesis.* Chicago: Aldine, 1974.

Taietz, P. "Conflicting Group Norms and the 'Third Person' in the Interview." *American Journal of Sociology,* 1962, *68,* 97–104.

Terman, L. M. *Psychological Factors of Marital Happiness.* New York: McGraw-Hill, 1938.

Tukey, J. W. "One Degree of Freedom for Non-Additivity." *Biometrics,* 1949, *5,* 232–242.

U.S. Brewers Association, Inc. *The Brewing Industry in the United States: Brewers Almanac 1975.* Washington, D.C.: U.S. Brewers Association, 1975.

U.S. National Center for Health Services Research. *Experiments in Interviewing Techniques.* NCHSR Research Report, 78-7. Hyattsville, Md.: U.S. National Center for Health Services Research, 1977.

Warner, S. L. "Randomized Response: A Survey Technique for Eliminating Error Answer Bias." *Journal of the American Statistical Association,* 1965, *60,* 63–69.

Warwick, D. P. "Social Scientists Ought to Stop Lying." *Psychology Today,* 1975, *8,* 38.

Weiss, C. "Validity of Welfare Mothers' Interview Responses." *Public Opinion Quarterly,* 1968, *32,* 622–633.

Wildman, R. C. "Effects of Anonymity and Social Setting on Survey Responses." *Public Opinion Quarterly,* 1977, *41,* 74–79.

Wilson, W. C. "The Distribution of Selected Sexual Attitudes and Behaviors Among the Adult Population of the United States." *Journal of Sex Research,* 1975, *11,* 46–64.

Index

209